The
Mediocrity
Of
Education system

A must Read for Students

Raghav Goyal

"For the students who want to know the truth of Education System"

"For the students who don't want be mediocre anymore"

"For the students who now want to wake up and do something in life"

"Education is not the learning of facts, but the training of the mind to think."
– Albert Einstein

"Do not confine your children to your own learning, for they were born in another time."
– Chinese Proverb

"The purpose of education is to replace an empty mind with an open one."
– Malcolm Forbes

"The mind is not a vessel to be filled, but a fire to be kindled."
– Plutarch

Contents

Introduction

Unit 1: *The history of Education System*

Ch-1 : *The Evolution of education*

Ch-2 : *The shift from wisdom to workforce*

Unit 2: *Present day education system*

Ch-3 : *The transformation of education from purpose driven to profit making*

Ch-4 : *Marks and Unhealthy Competition*

Ch-5 : *Superficial thinking and limited learning*

Ch-6 : *Teachers and Exploitation*

Ch-7 : *The murder of practical knowledge*

Unit 3: *The students perspective*

Ch-8 : *The modern experience of students in this system*

Ch-9 : *Early career decisions*

Ch-10 : *The Reality of "Learning" today*

Ch-11 : *The role of coaching classes and institutions*

Unit 4: *The role of Parents*

Ch-12 : *Parenting and Education*

Ch-13 : *Under parenting VS Over parenting*

Ch-14 : *Providing emotional support and creating and learning environment*

Unit 5: *The Rat Race/Matrix*

Ch-15 : *What the hell is Rat Race?*

Ch-16 : *The system training you for this trap*

Ch-17 : *Breaking the chains of mediocrity*

Unit 6 : *The role of government in education*

Ch-18 : *The flawed governmental foundation*

Ch-19 : *Uneducated leaders and misguided policies*

Ch-20 : *The mediocre Curriculum*

Unit 7 : *The Solutions*

Ch-21 : *The global model for education*

Ch-22 : *The changes needed in the Education system*

Ch-23 : *The mindset shift in Parents, Society and Students itself*

The End Thoughts

Introduction

Imagine a world where no one knows how to read or write.

There are no books, no way to communicate ideas beyond speaking . Knowledge becomes limited to what can be passed down through stories and much of the world remains a mystery. There are no engineers, no doctors, no teachers or business men and there is only the vague wisdom of those before us.

In this type of world, every invention, every advancement in technology, science, and the arts halts.

Society stagnates.

 How do we solve problems, innovate, or progress without education to guide us?

Even the simplest of tasks like , understanding a map, following directions, or reading a warning sign become an impossible task.
In such a world, chaos would reign.

Without the ability to learn, share knowledge, and teach ; humanity would lose its most powerful tool which is the power to think .

The ability to think critically, solve problems, and imagine new possibilities would be lost. That's what life would be like without education: not hopeful or encouraging but stagnant, and without hope for progress and develop.

The importance of education

Education, in its truest of form, is not just about getting a degree or getting a job. It is about expanding the horizons of the human mind.

Education builds societies, shapes economies, and fosters innovation. It is that which keeps us moving forward as a civilization and species.

Without education, we would not be able to decode the mysteries of the universe or harness the power of technology to improve our lives and develop further.

Every major breakthrough, from the discovery of electricity to the creation of the internet, has its roots in education. But it is more than just the academic learning.

Education empowers us to understand our rights to be informed citizens to challenge injustices and to create a better world.

Like, Oprah Winfrey, one of the most influential media person in the world, often speaks about her educational journey which is like this.

She growed up in poverty, she attended a well-funded public high school in Nashville and she tells that "Education is what saved me," she says it opened up a new world of possibilities for me because of which I am the one who I should be.

But at the same an interesting part comes about education and education system.
Now here her success underscores the impact that access to quality education can have on a person's life and what is the importance of education.It education that allows us to grow. It shapes our morals, guides our every decision that we take and builds our character.

Education is not just a right but it's actually the foundation on which every other right is built of a human. It is what that helps us to be better individuals and, in turn, build better communities.

The reality of today's education system

Now a question; do our current education system is like what we are reading about?

Well, that's about the journey of this book that I want you to travel with me.

Still, despite a very important role that education plays in our lives, today's system often falls short of its promises and values.

In the modern world, education has sometimes become more about ticking boxes, passing tests, getting degrees and following routines rather than truly learning and becoming what you want to.

Students are being pushed to memorize facts, rather than understanding the "Why" and the "How" behind them.

Teachers who are overwhelmed by standardized systems, struggle to inspire the creativity and critical thinking that true education should actually create.

We have come to measure success through grades and test scores, but what about the development of our curious mind?

What about teaching students to think, question, and innovate?

The original goal of education was to open minds and develop lifelong learners, but somewhere along that way, we have lost that focus.

Why does this book matter?

This book is not just a critique of the current system but it's a call to action.

It's a guide to rethinking how we approach education, to valuing creativity, critical thinking, and real-world problem-solving over rote memorization and conformity.

It's about shifting our focus back to what truly matters and preparing students for life, not just for exams.

Throughout this book, we will explore real-life stories of individuals who have succeeded not because of traditional education, but in spite of it.

We'll look at innovative education models that are already reshaping the way we learn. And we'll challenge the assumptions we hold about what education should be.

We will cover every aspect of this system that are society, parents , students, teachers and the government.

From the history to current education system and the perspective of students to parents and government, every single thing has an impact on this system and we will cover that all.

I am sure that most of the books that you have read till now might be the one in which in starting you are excited and able to read it with a hit but as the book continues, you start loosing interest.

But here in this book the case in just the opposite of it, in starting you can still feel not that energetic but as the journey will continue, you will get more and more into it.

By the end, my hope as "student" itself to you is , the reader, will have a renewed understanding of what education can be , an empowering, enriching force that equips us to change the world but today it's something different and a change is needed.

Because in the end, education is not about teaching facts; it's about fostering a love for learning, a curiosity for the unknown, and the skills to transform ideas into reality.

So read till the end!

Let's get started.

Unit 1: The history of education system
Ch -1 The Evolution of Education

I want to ask you that Education as we know today, was it always like this? Was it always similar like this? And the answer is of course No.

Their is a long way that education has travelled over the centuries.

The journey has got a lot of changes in between it which has shaped this system.

This journey from the wisdom driven education system of the ancient civilizations to today's modern and standardized education system is a story of both ups and downs, and growth and losses ,which mainly was of down and losses.

Now a question , do these shifts and changes has shaped us?

 And the answer is; YES.

While education has expanded a lot to reach millions of people like us, in some ways, it has also narrowed its focus by moving away from true wisdom and personal growth to preparing individuals for the workforce and labour.

The origins of education

The Education served in the ancient times was not at all same as of today, that time the education was practical, personalized, and also it was deeply rooted with the values and morals of our community.

At that time it wasn't merely about memorizing facts or exceptions, or even preparing for tests or exams. It was mainly about getting up with the next generation of wisdom to survive, thrive and contribute something meaningful to the society by upgrading yourself at the same time.

In the prehistoric times, education was informal which was passed from one generation to another by the oral teaching which were guided by own parents and elders of the child.

They taught the children about the essential skills needed for survival such as hunting, gathering, tool-making, and understanding the natural world.

This early education was integrated with daily life and immediate needs, by students learning directly from their experiences, mistakes and their community.

As the civilizations formed, education became more formalized and this started changing this system.

Like, In ancient Egypt, education was closely tied to religious and administrative functions. Scribes, who were highly educated in writing and record-keeping, played very critical roles in managing the affairs of the state.

Something similarly, in Greece, education was aimed at producing well-rounded citizens which would be capable of contributing to the public life.

The great philosophers, such as Socrates and Plato, emphasized reasoning, critical thinking and the pursuit of knowledge as the highest form of education.

India's Ancient Gurukul System

One of the most revered ancient education systems was India's Gurukul system, where education was more than just about acquiring knowledge but it was a way of life.

Students, or "shishyas," lived with their teachers, or "gurus," in small communities that were often situated in remote and natural settings.
The teacher-student relationship was central to the learning process, and it was one of respect, humility, and personal development.

This system was so rich with different types of subjects like maths, science, philosophy, astronomy, agriculture, medicine, yoga, Martial arts, weaponry, politics, governance, music, art and many more.

The main point is not only in these subjects but how that were taught and how the students got it.

The education was highly personalized in this system. The Gurus would understand the unique abilities, strengths, and interests of each student and guide them accordingly.

There were no mass classrooms, standardized tests, or rigid curriculum. Instead, students learned at their own pace, and their learning was driven by curiosity and a deep bond with their teacher.

One of the most striking aspects of the Gurukul system was its emphasis on applying knowledge.

The students didn't just learn theories; they practiced what they learned through hands-on experience.

Whether it was learning how to grow crops, solve complex mathematical problems, or recite ancient hymns, education was just a process of mastery through practice and learning from the hands on experiences and mistakes.

There were more systems in the past similar to the Gurukul system like Confucian education system of China, French education system, Academies of Greece, Indigenous education system of Northern and Western Africa, Zen Monastic of Japan and so on.

At that time in past everything was well sorted with students and teachers where they were both happy and there was healthy learning, but slowly as the population growed, some people of society become powerful and rich , they started bringing changes in the education systems for their benefit. This was the time when when the changes start taking place in the society.

What were they?

Let's see and find it out in the next chapter.

Chapter 2
The shift from wisdom to workforce

We now know as the societies changed and industrialized , the nature and the working of education totally changed.

The advent of the Industrial Revolution brought with its need for a disciplined, literate workforce to run factories, manage production, and fuel the growing economy .

Governments began to implement standardised education systems to meet these needs, and schools became institutions that were designed to produce workers rather than thinkers.

Today's Education System

The mass education system we know today was originated in the 19th century and it was heavily influenced by the needs of industrial economies.

With the rise of factories and industries, the demand for a workforce with basic literacy and numeracy skills became important, who would mainly listen the orders given to them by their bosses without even questioning once.

Thus, the schools were established to instill these fundamental skills in large groups of children to make them labours and produce a loyal workforce who can work without using their own brains and just work by what is said to them, just like a puppet.

How was this system established ?

Now as we are clear with how such changes started taking place, now a question comes how was it established and when?

The formation of this mediocre system took place when in 19th century, the war between Prussian army and the army of Napoleon took place.

In this War, the Prussian army was more in number than of the Napoleon army but still Napoleon won.

After the war, all the leaders- superior heads started thinking how they have lost even after having such a big army, then some of the leaders from them found out, they were having a strong and big army but still we lost because the soldiers were not listening to us (to the leaders) and they were doing the fight at their own by using their own brains , basically they were not listening the orders of their leaders.

On the other hand, Napoleon's army was listening the orders of Napoleon. As a result , the Prussia had to give their half of territory to Napoleon and sign a peace agreement.

To make sure that this will not happen in the future again, after this they started thinking to prevent this for the future and solve the problem and after some time they came up with an idea to establish a system in which the soldiers will be trained only that much that they should listen the orders of seniors without thinking at their own.
And how this would become successful?, by controlling the young minds who have not grown and developed yet.

This took place by establishing a education system - Prussian education system , in this system the school of 8 years was made compulsory for the children aged 5 to 13.

The soul purpose of this system was to train the people just to obey and follow the rules of their seniors and never think big by doing something at their own and without even questioning the system.

Well before this system till now their were basic conversation, debates between the teachers (educators) and learners(students) in the system , but after this system and in this system, textbooks were also introduced as a main source of education, which at some point substituted the teachers.

This is something that you can also find today that if you are reading and learning something from your books at your own, you would still get a idea, or learn something of it , but in past when there were no books mainly in the teaching there was a need of teachers and always students were allowed to question everything ; but after this that was not a point because even the teachers were also trained from the same system.

Coming back, the leaders as planned, got successful in their plan and they continued the same system , the soldiers were listening to them.

And like this - A system was established !

How this system from Prussia got exported to the world ?

At the same time of this system , the industrialization was rapidly evolving, and at that time in factories labourers were needed to work .

So just because how hit was this system, this was in the limelight and in the eyes of big industry people.

Now they also started taking actions to develop a system in their countries with the main motive of making the children labourers by killing their creativity and critical thinking skills.
Like, A billionaire Industrialist also known as 1st billionaire of the world of United States of America, John D Rockefeller, also started to implement a similar system in US as he wanted workers to work in his factories and Oil refineries to handle his oil empire.

His problem was also that he was not getting loyal workers to work in his factories and refineries as whenever he employed workers they always got off from their by escaping them because in past at that time they were also knowing that this will be a slavery and if we want to do work we can do at our own like farming or making paintings, potries etc.

This was the reason that John D started making a similar system like Prussian Education System in USA.

He copied the same by implementing it for the same group of children and with same pace, for the same, In US he made the parents of children believe that this is a way of success for your children and if you will send them to schools they will be rich enough in the future.

He made them also think that education is really important because in past illiterate people were even earning that much by doing something that they can still live with it, but just in chase of money and success, also the parents and children in US got into this trap and they ruined their future.

Then after this, he made the schools at that time totally free of cost, where he provided the students only this much of knowledge that was needed for the students to become an loyal worker by mainly implementing a very mediocre system of teaching and making goals for them to make them just on them to which we today know as Syllabus .

And similarly, his plan also got successful and he earned high profits as people were working in his factories without complaining.

Slowly- Slowly this same system started travelling the world and big people started adopting it to make others poor and middle class.

After this, the same system started implementing in other countries by the powerful people of the society for their benefits.

But the main turning point and a big role in being implemented in almost every good country, was of British Empire.

Similarly the British wanted workforce to work under them in a similar way.

At their best, they got the most of it, in a very short period of time, with their importance , they got a really huge success in India.

How did the British influenced this system?

Now after this as the British also wanted workforce to work under them and similarly they weren't getting loyal workforce like John D Rockefeller to work for them, they also started implementing this same type of system in the countries they ruled at that time.

Some of 1st countries were the African and Carribean countries but that was not something that really contributed to them as an Empire because of the small size of the population and not getting anything much valuable in that countries for trade.

So from where Really this System was a Big Hit (disaster), by which we all are following this system today?

First, the primary role in this was of British for sure, but the Country where they implemented it was India , due to its large size, population and valuable goods for trade.

Just because of this they started to make changes in the education system of India at a such extand just because they wanted loyal workforce, they actually changed the whole education system of India, which is still followed till today's date and moreover if a Indian today says "Indian" education system to name it
so, actually it's not the "Indian" Education system but the "British education system".

The main purpose of this system was to shut down the brains of the indian and make them to follow every instruction without questioning it and live a rule based life.

How it got implemented and changed the whole India which further shaped the education systems of the world ?

So, I want to tell you that ,if you think this system was implemented by the whole British Empire so, I want to clear it like a glass for you that the British Empire was such a big Empire with a lot of leaders in it, so the duty to change the old education system of India was given to a new one, it was given to one person to whom you might know as you might have read about him in your History Textbooks , he was *"Thomas Babington Macaulay"*

So, Macaulay's policy, "A Minute on Education" That was introduced in 1835 was the policy that changed the whole education system by shifting towards a system where English education in India was made mandatory for all the students.

The main goal of this system was to make a pool of Indians who would be able to serve to Britishers and the local population,without questioning and asking them any thing extra.

Before this system India was so rich in education, as India had the gurukul system about which we talked in the previous chapters, because of this system Indians were so rich in knowledge and culture, but this British system killed India.

The literacy rate before British colonialism in India is estimated to have been as high as 97%, a reflection of the effectiveness of gurukul education model but on the other hand after this system it dropped down to 80% just in a few years and in the 20th century the average rate was considered as only 45-52% and now it is (as of present 2022) record still it is 76% only, just see the difference.

Just because everything changed in 1835 when Thomas Babington Macaulay, a British politician and historian, implemented the colonial/British education system in India.

Macaulay's infamous Minute on Education laid the groundwork for an education system that would serve the British Empire's needs, not India's.

His goal was to produce a class of people who were, in his own words, "Indian in blood and colour, but English in taste, in opinions, in morals, and in intellect", which means creating a class of Indians who look Indian but think, act, and behave like the British by adopting British values, culture, and mindset while abandoning their own heritage and culture, also they behave like British not means like an officer or smart man, but actually a puppet .

To achieve this, Macaulay promoted a Westernized curriculum that emphasized English language and literature also the core subjects in this was crambing and only understanding the things that are already their and nothing at you own even when in this system subjects like Science, Mathematics and social science existed ,while dismissing the rich heritage of Indian knowledge.

He went so far as to claim that "a single shelf of a good European library was worth the whole native literature of India and Arabia."

This phrase was totally meant to disrespect the Indian culture and wisdom ,which was the driving force behind the introduction of a new system that would focus more on rote memorization and blind obedience than on nurturing critical thinkers and innovators.

This system was basically far more rigid and mechanical, which just focused on modern industrial revolutional factory system.

Standardized curricular, rigid timetables, and a hierarchical teacher-student dynamic were introduced in this system just to ensure that students learned not to question authority but to follow orders.

Even Do you remember that bell in your school which was rung after every period when the period gets over or schools gets over?

That bell was also made by Britishers only.

They made this that students should start following their rules and regulations from a young age and become a slave of the timetable and schedule, basically in this system "Obedience" Was meant as the true "Discipline".

In actuall, the system was not designed to educate free-thinking individuals but to produce obedient, English-speaking clerks who could help administer British rule in India.

Then the this System started traveling the world

After this, Macaulay's influence did not stop with India.

The British Empire imposed similar education systems across its colonies in Africa, the Caribbean, and Southeast Asia.

These systems were not tailored to the needs or cultures of the local populations, instead they were designed to produce colonial subjects who could help in maintaining British rule.

In India, Macaulay's policies were particularly successful in creating a class of educated Indians who could serve as intermediaries between the British rulers and the local population and something similar was in other colonies also.

What impact did this system had on the world?

The impact of this education system is still felt on the world where most of the countries especially Indian countries like India, Pakistan and Bangladesh are still following the same rigid circular

Fast forward to the 21st century, and many of these characteristics remain central to modern education systems, even though the world has shifted from an industrial economy to a knowledge-based one but, still it is the same.

Most education systems are still highly standardized which emphasizing conformity, rote memorization, and examinations.

The idea that students should be "products" designed for specific roles within the economy remains strong, despite evidence suggesting that creativity, critical thinking, and adaptability are the skills most needed in today's rapidly changing world.

And after the lasting World War ll, the education system became even more standardized and cruel for the students.

The impact of world War ll

After World War I and II, nations around the world sought to further strengthen their education systems to rebuild economies and foster national unity.

This push for standardized education expanded globally, particularly after World War II when both the U.S. and Soviet Union emphasized the importance of
science, technology, and obedience in schools to compete with each other in the Cold War.

These horrors of the wars , shattered much of the global infrastructure, and then their, education was seen as a vital tool for recovery and progress.

Governments recognized that schools could be used to create a unified, loyal citizenry that would contribute to national development and could recover the loss.

At the end, Both the superpowers saw education as a means to prepare future generations for competition in global arenas, particularly in space exploration and military technology.

The focus on obedience, standardized testing, and uniformity across school systems was viewed as essential for fostering disciplined, industrious citizens who could support national agendas and again work for the benefits of government.

The shift towards standardized and industrialized education systems after World War I and II didn't solved the problem or reduced it, but it actually exacerbated the problem even more .

As nations rebuilt and sought to maintain power and legacy of the country, schools became even more rigid, focused solely on producing a compliant workforce rather than fostering creativity or critical thinking of the students .

This system, rooted in the needs of war time economies and later Cold War competition, prioritized conformity over individuality and obedience over innovation.

As a result, generations of students worldwide were conditioned to fit into predefined roles rather than encourage to challenge the status quo or think independently.

The aftermath of these wars not only solidified the factory model of education, but also it perpetuated a global crisis where true learning was sacrificed for uniformity, leaving us with an outdated system that no longer serves the needs of a rapidly evolving world".

Unit 2 The present day education system
Ch 3 The transformation of education from purpose driven to profit making

I want to ask a question from you all, the education system that we discussed in chapter 1 of the book, and the education served today, are they both the same?
Well, the answer isn't that tough to answer , that is No .

As in earlier times the education hailed as the pilliar of the society which was necessity for everyone and was served free or at very low costs, but today education isn't the same at all.

The average inflation in India is 6% annually on the other hand, average inflation in the education sector in India is around 11-12% annually . Almost double the average inflation!

An Average middle class or even an normal person in India sees education as an investment as we discussed in chapter 2, for them the priority is sending their child to one of the top school of their city , with a dream of that their child will not face and live the same life as of theirs but actually the difference is same, that there is not a big difference.

The education earlier, was originally built upon the foundation of enlightenment and empowerment.

It provided a means to unlock the potential of individuals, to educate, and to foster critical thinking. But , the purpose of education began to shift, which was once a system designed to build minds has now become a machine that prioritizes profit over knowledge, competition over collaboration, and surface-level achievement over true understanding.

Fast forward to todays life, we see a very different reality in front of our eyes.
Education has morphed into a corporate-driven industry, with the rise of private schools, universities, and expensive coaching institutes.

The noble ideals of learning for growth, wisdom, and enlightenment have been overshadowed by the business models that treats students as customers and education as the product.

The goal now, is no longer the pursuit of knowledge for the betterment of society but, the pursuit of profit for institutional gain.

There are two main pillars of this education system that has become today , they are 'Good Marks' and "Completion of Syllabus".

These pillars are the main pillars to which the schools say the foundation of this system.

See if the Base of a building is only shit then how can the building be a building and we can build a building or if build how can it last for long time.

Whereas the two pillars should be 'Skill set ' and 'Knowledge' of the education institutions, today it's just something the opposite of it.

The Rise of Private Schools

One of the most visibles signs of the same is the Private Schools today.

Earlier, schools were primarily run by the guru or person who really wants to teach, state or by charitable organizations that sought to educate the masses with no goal of earning big profits, especially those who couldn't afford education otherwise.

However, with the rise of private institutions, education has become a commodity accessible only to those who can afford it.

Private schools advertise themselves as places of quality education, promising state-of-the-art facilities, excellent teachers, and better prospects for the future.
But at what cost?

For many families, these promises come with steep fees, sometimes out of reach for them.

Parents are often pressured to invest large sums of money into these schools, believing that this is the only way their children can succeed in life.

The commercial nature of education has led to a situation where money, not merit, often determines the quality of education a student receives.
Like for an average Indian Family, private schools are everything, like they want thier child to get the best form of education from these schools, but actually it isn't.

Every year these school take fees from the parents for no purpose with contrast of different names. Like Annual and Admission fees is raised every year in the schools, but the teachers working in the school still work on the same salary.

And other fees like Library, smart class, computer class, every year these all the fees are raised but still there are always the same books in library, same smart class and computers that work like that are from 2nd Generation.

Every month these all sort of different charges are taken but this is only sometimes that we go or use the equipments in the school.

Even the government knows all of this but still they don't take action because they all want that most of the things and services of the country should go in the private hands so that they can spend the tax money for their security and pleasure.

Will like this, will be able to make our nation educated or literate? Still, The illiteracy rate of the country is more than 24%.

Education as a Business

The shift to profit-oriented education is perhaps most evident in the rise of elite universities and coaching institutions.

By the education becoming more competitive, particularly in our country India, coaching centers have sprung up to cater to students desperate to crack prestigious exams such as the IIT-JEE or medical entrance exams like NEET or the civil services such as UPSC.

These coaching centers promise results, but at very big amount of fees which creates a highly lucrative market for educators and corporations.

Education has become a multi-billion dollar industry, with both schools and universities fighting for top rankings and students eager to pay for the privilege of attending these institutions.

As it is recorded that global education market is of around 506 Billions and alone in India around 105 Billions.
As a result?

Education has lost its inner soul for which it was truly ment to be. Instead of creating an environment for intellectual curiosity and personal growth, it has created a system that churns out students focused solely on marks and rankings, and job prospects.

The broader goal of education , to develop well-rounded individuals
capable of critical thinking and contributing to society has taken a
backseat.

Also coming to the context of collages, it is recorded that there are more
than 40,000 collages in India but, out of that only 10-15 are relevant, which
creates a sense of herd mentality of going to the best colleges and working
hard to crack the entrance exam.

The examples are super easy and are in front of you as a student who wants
to do engineering goes for IIT and medical students for AIIMS.

The True cost of profit driven education

The consequences of this transformation are dire. In the race of profits, the
system has lost its purpose.

Students are now treated as consumers and they are pushed through the
system with little regard for personal development.

They are taught to memorize, not to question. To pass exams, not to think
critically. This has stifled creativity, curiosity, and the ability to innovate.
Moreover, the burden on students and their families is immense.
In this profit-oriented model, education is no longer the empowering force
which was once meant to be.

Instead, it has become a source of stress, anxiety, and even resentment.

Students feel pressured to conform to a system that values rote learning
over intellectual exploration, and parents are left with the financial strain
of trying to secure their children's futures.

Can we reclaim the purpose of education ?

The transformation of education from purpose-free to profit-oriented is
perhaps one of the greatest tragedies of our time. Today it has become a

corporate enterprise driven by money and power. But still there is some hope.

There is a growing awareness of the flaws in the current system, and calls for reform are gaining momentum. If we can reclaim the true purpose of education
– to empower, enlighten, and inspire – we may yet be able to reverse the damage and create a system that benefits all, not just the privileged few.

The question now is: will we act? , or will we continue to let education fall deeper into the hands of those who see it only as a profit-making machine?

Chapter 4 Marks and Unhealthy competition

The Modern education system of today's world , with its intense focus on marks and academic competition between students/peers has created an environment where students are valued not for their knowledge or critical thinking skills, but for their ability to score high in exams.

This shift has led several changes in the eco system like unhealthy competition between students, the stifling of curiosity, and the promotion of superficial learning.
So in this chapter, we will explore how this unhealthy race for marks has killed the very essence of learning and turned education into a mechanical process devoid of exploration, creativity, or true understanding.

The rise of marks as the sole aim of success

Now, just a question to you all, have you even experienced the punch of marks from parents, teachers and the society? Like get good marks and marks. I am sure you all might have . But what this has brought to our system?

Like in today's education system, marks are not just numbers they have become a medium for this system to define the worth of a student.

The higher the students score, the greater the recognition and appreciation. This marks-centric culture began taking root as schools started aligning themselves more with the needs of industrialized economies and emphasizing standardized testing and measurable outcomes over meaningful education. But what happens when marks become the sole objective?

Some are the ones who are able to get it (marks), but some not and the worst part of this is that it has created a problem which is not a joke, but a real serious problem.

The claim is even that suicide is a leading cause of death among students and young people aged 14 to 24 .

According to various studies, suicide is one of the top causes of death for this age group globally, with increasing trends in many regions.
In the United States, for instance, suicide rates among individuals aged 15 to 24 have significantly risen over the years. In 2022, the suicide rate for this age group was reported at 5.8 per 100,000 people, up from 2.9 per 100,000 in 2002.

In India, suicide is a significant public health issue, particularly among adolescents and young adults.

According to a 2021 analysis, suicide is the leading cause of death for individuals aged 15 to 29 in India.

The National Crime Records Bureau (NCRB) reported that in 2021, over 134,000 people died by suicide in the country.

Among these, the age group of 15 to 29 accounted for the highest percentage of deaths.

Over the past decade, the suicide rate among children and adolescents in India has risen significantly, especially after 2014. In 2021, nearly 10,730 adolescents between the ages of 10 to 19 died by suicide.

Students are taught that their success, future opportunities, and self-worth hinge on their ability to outperform others in exams. As a result, learning takes a back seat, and the desire to gain knowledge is replaced by the need to secure high marks at any cost.

On the other hand as we disscused in ancient times like ancient India's 'gurukul system', the aim was on learning and improving yourself but today because of the eco system of the system, this has changed totally.

If a student is the one who is not able to obtain good marks, the society and all treat him like that he is a looser and because of this the students also start questioning their spirits.

Even Albert Einstein said that if you will judge a fish by its ability to climb a tree and not by swim in water, the fish will always belive that it is a looser. This basically means that everyone is unique on its own, everyone is special in something, they are good in something in which others are not.

But the system of marks is all killing it because even the person who is not good at scoring higher marks is treated like a looser.

And also I have to story to share with you all about this, like of you think
that even the top scientist and Geniuses of the world were like the one
scoring really good marks, then this story might shock you, which even
shocked me after I read it.

Isaac Newton wasn't the kind of student that you might expect to change
the course of history.

He was born in 1642, he was sent away to school, where he struggled to fit
in within this system.
His teachers didn't see much potential in him, and Newton himself wasn't
inspired by the rigid and uninspiring teaching methods. He found the
classroom boring, and while his peers played during recess he would sit
under a tree and lost in his dreams

It wasn't that Newton couldn't learn; he just didn't thrive in an
environment that stifled creativity.

He was deeply curious, but the formal education system didn't nurture
that. In fact, at one point, he was removed from school to help in his family
farm, as his mother didn't think education was for him or children like
him. Yet, his mind was restless.

Away from the structured classroom, Newton's curiosity flourished. He
began conducting experiments in secret and developed his understanding in
the natural world through observations. That boy who couldn't fit into the
traditional system then went on to define the laws of gravity, motion, and
invent calculus. All things that profoundly shape our world today and we
all study in our school time!

Imagine what might have happened if Newton had remained confined to
that strict, boring classrooms.

If his curiosity had been crushed, if he had never explored beyond the walls
of formal education, the world might never have known the brilliance that
lay within him.

Like Newton, Albert Einstein wasn't the kind of student you'd expect to become one of the most influential physicists of all time.
Born in 1879, he didn't speak until the age of three, and his teachers often thought he was slow, a daydreamer, and someone who didn't quite fit in the people.

In school, Einstein was often frustrated by the rote memorization that the education system demanded.

His mind worked differently.
He wasn't content with simply absorbing information but he wanted to question everything, to understand how and why things worked.

His teachers, however, were more focused on obedience and memorization than on nurturing that curiosity that he had. Einstein skipped classes, preferring to learn at his own pace by often reading books that were not assigned by his teachers.

His report cards were not impressive, and many considered him a lost cause academically.

But outside the classroom, Einstein was unstoppable. He spent hours imagining complex scenarios like what would it be like to ride alongside a beam of light?
This question, born of pure curiosity, eventually led to his theory of relativity, forever changing our understanding of the universe.

If Einstein had remained within the constraints of traditional schooling, his mind might have been dulled. Instead, he thrived because he refused to let the system define his potential. The very same system that deemed him a failure could not comprehend the brilliance that resided in his unconventional way of thinking.

Now these both stories shows how sometimes, those who appear to be "failures" within the system have the greatest potential when allowed to think freely and question the world around them. Also the main point is the actually that so called 'marks', that are seen as a unit to measure success in schools is nothing, but just some numbers.

Unhealthy Competition

Now again, I want to ask you all have your parents, teachers, relatives or the society compared you with others studying with you?

The answer might be the same as 'yes', and it is. So what, why this is? Like, Compitition is good but not good for how much you know and for the marks. Here is a compitition for getting 99% marks which is not at all good.

And after this also when students don't get success. It's more sad and just due to this a further big problem is created which is of suicides.

These marks and acedmics have developed a toxic environment for the students/peers/friends. They just standout as a rival against each other sometimes when it comes to marks, but why? Why they are not forced to actually help each other and create a win-win situation, where if a one student
knows something but other not, so why the one knowing help his friends and peers?

Just because of this, Instead of collaborating, sharing ideas, and learning together, students are pitted against each other in a never-ending battle for academic superiority.

Just think like this only that in the exam Hall you all have been given the same problems to solve and you all working entirely for marks and completing against each other. Instead of a system, an exam can be made where you all are working on the same problem to solve it. This is simply an example of hands on learning.

Like this even if then students are given ranks on the basis of teams , that is too good to be good.
And just tell me or see around you, have you ever seen a person building a company, business on its own?

All the ones who create they collaborate, share ideas and learn together to build a superb work.

One country that exemplifies that this can be fixed is the education system of Finland. In Finnish schools, the focus is not on competition, but on collaboration and holistic development. There are no standardized tests until the end of high school, and students are encouraged to learn at their own pace.

 The emphasis is on fostering critical thinking, creativity, and a genuine love of learning.

Finnish students consistently rank among the top in global education assessments, yet they spend less time in the classroom and experience far less stress than their counterparts in other countries. The Finnish model demonstrates that when the pressure to compete is removed, students can thrive academically and personally.

From an early age only, students are conditioned to believe that success is measured by their ability to outperform their peers in exams. The entire educational journey, from primary school to college, is a series of hurdles designed to sort and rank students based on their academic performance.

 This competitive atmosphere fosters a mindset where the primary goal is not learning, but winning.

And tell me, is learning means winning or really learning? Is the things taught in school, taught on the basis of learning or competing with each other?

Sundar Pichai, now the CEO of Alphabet Inc. and Google, faced the same academic pressures that countless students around the world experience. Born in Tamil Nadu, India, Pichai grew up in a system that emphasized marks and competition, often measuring success by exam scores rather than true learning.

In school, Pichai was an excellent student, but like many others, he was surrounded by a culture where success was often defined solely by academic rankings.

While he did well in his studies, Pichai later shared that his journey wasn't about competing for marks but about genuine interest in problem-solving and learning. Rather than focusing on grades, Pichai found that his curiosity and passion for technology were what ultimately shaped his path to success.

He once shared how growing up in a modest home with limited resources shaped his appreciation for learning rather than competing for the sake of marks.

When he later attended IIT Kharagpur, a premier engineering institution, the competition was fierce. However, Pichai continued to follow his passion, excelling not because of the competition but because he found joy in innovation and exploration.

His journey stands as a reminder that curiosity and the desire to solve real-world problems are far more valuable than being stuck in the unhealthy competition of chasing marks.

Ch 5 Superficial thinking and limited learning

I want to ask you all how the schools are today?

Might like this?
The classes start usually at 7:30 and then there is assembly in the school
after that there is attendance and like this the boring lectures of 40 minutes
each start in the school which end at 2:00.

In the class half of the students pay attention half not.

After 3 months, there are exams and one day before exam everyone studies
and eats everything that is in the book then just throws off at vomits in the
exam and then they get their results if pass - happy and if fail - sad.

And this is how the fucking pattern goes on and on.
Now think; As marks become the goal, students are conditioned to study
only what is necessary to score well and not gain more information and
knowledge,which is necessary for them,like it is made to be a belief that
whatever is written in the textbook, is real.

This limited approach to education results in shallow understanding and
fragmented knowledge. Instead of nurturing thinkers and problem-solvers
this system create rote learners.

And this too you might have experienced, if something comes in your school
exam from a bit outside of the textbook or it is a bit complex , then the
students start complaining that it's out of syllabus, this is just because that
you only read and learn what is in the book , because actually the topic is
same, only there are some slight new things that you haven't read, and you
fail to answer it.

The main problem is that, that we are trained to remember things and not
understand them and learn them.

Also see, as we disscused about ancient education systems, there were not
same systems like this, to just learn a piece of something for the sake of
marks.

Students were really educated and creative, they were innovative.

And this is something that you can now see in the context of India like in part there are numerous innovations that we have done, like the discovery of Zero, button, plastic surgery, Ayurveda and many more but now we are not able to figure out what exactly there is.

Like before the colonial rule India ranked at Number 1 when it comes to innovation, but after the colonial rule we ranked at 100 and today we are still at 40th..

The sad truth is that most of what they "learn" is quickly forgotten once the test is over. What remains is a fragmented understanding, a hollow sense of knowledge that does nothing to foster real intellectual growth.

This system always fails to encourage students to be curious or to develop a passion for learning, creating a generation that knows how to pass exams but not how to think critically about the world.

Perhaps even more damaging is how this marks-driven system kills critical thinking.

Students aren't rewarded for asking hard questions, for challenging what they're taught, or for exploring a topic from a new angle. Instead, they're taught to stick to the script , give the 'right' answer, fit within the framework of the exam, and move on to the next class.

Also this lack of practicall learning causes more problems.

Like I have seen one more thing in this education system and that is repeated to the lack of practicall learning in the whole subject that is 100% practical , that are the language subjects like English and Hindi.
Just think, why we need these things as subjects, just need it for the communication purpose and in that too if the schools are using it as subjects to attain marks and not to actually teach students how to speak effectively then?

Like in my school there are my friends with me who take part in public speaking competitions, they are really good at spoken English, but if talking about their english grammar exam then it is not to good.
But do this means that they don't know how to speak English?
No. Not at all. They know English better than that toppers too.

Like there are that so called toppers in my class only who can score full marks in English but they cannot speak English effectively.

And the same story goes around Hindi.
Creativity is stifled because the system values conformity. To make matters worse, making mistakes which was once seen as a natural part of learning is now treated as failure.

The fear of losing marks or being labeled as 'wrong' discourages students from taking intellectual risks, trying out new ideas, or pushing the boundaries of their understanding.

Over time, this creates a culture where mistakes aren't learning opportunities but roadblocks. And with that, the very essence of curiosity—the spark that drives innovation and meaningful discovery—is lost.

And even just to check about this cramb mentality and limited thinking, I asked my 5 different friends about how many seasons (weather) are in India and out of them 2 answered that there are 4 seasons in India which are spring, autumn, summer and winter, then 3 answered 5 by adding a monsoon season. But these both answers were not correct because actually in India there are 6 different weather seasons.

They were answering the wrong one because they have never known with real knowledge and have just learned what was in their text books.

The six seasons are actually Summer, Winter, Monsoon, spring, autumn and pre- winter.

And this is the system in which we are currently studying today.

The true cost of this approach is enormous.

We're not just stunting the growth of individuals but limiting the potential of society as a whole.
By discouraging curiosity and critical thinking, we are cutting off the pipeline of future thinkers, problem-solvers, and innovators.

In a world that desperately needs fresh ideas and bold solutions, this system is ensuring that most students never develop the skills or mindset to tackle the challenges ahead. We're raising generations that can follow instructions but not lead, people who can memorize but not create, and that is the greatest tragedy of all.

Even,Elon Musk, the founder of Tesla and SpaceX. He has frequently expressed his discontent with the way schools focus on rote learning and superficial understanding, limiting creativity and innovation.

He has shared his belief that the traditional education system is outdated and does not prepare students for real-world challenges.

He has mentioned that when he was in school, the rigid structure made it difficult to explore his interests. Despite being an excellent learner outside the classroom, Musk felt constrained by the system that emphasized grades and superficial learning over practical, hands-on problem-solving.

In fact, Musk founded Ad Astra, a private experimental school, to teach his children and a small group of other students in a way that encourages creativity, collaboration, and critical thinking. In this school, the focus is on learning

through doing and solving problems rather than memorizing facts. Musk believes that education should focus on developing skills like reasoning and curiosity, rather than simply preparing students to pass exams.

Ch 6 Teachers and Exploitation

Now as we are discussing the 'education system', So, how can we forget the ones who teach us - Teachers.

In education system teachers are always viewed as the backbone of the system, like from the past they are viewed as one of the highest priority in the system. They are the ones who are expected to shape the young minds, guide them, teach them, nature curiosity and fill lifetime values in them.

But today these teachers who are considered the backbone of the system are fractured (exploited) in the system by the system which leaves the students in a unhealthy place . But sometimes the teachers are the ones who leave the students there for their benefit, intentionally or with a loss of values and ethics in them.

What is the role of teachers? Are they just educators?

So, what do you think, are teachers just educators? Or they have a wide big role to play?

Well, they are the heart of the education, or just like the nucleus of a cell. They are not just the individuals who just impart knowledge, but also they are the mentors, role models, and the guides who help the students to navigate the complexities of life and learning.
They have the power to shape one, either by making him a hero or a loser.

Like, a good teacher can foster critical thinking, encourage curiosity, and push the students to explore beyond the textbook by their unique methods of teaching and the aura, on the other hand,there are some teachers who can just do opposite of it.

In an ideal world, teachers would have the time, energy, and resources to create a nurturing learning environment for every single student.

However, today's reality paints a different picture.

Teachers are overburdened with administrative work, oversized classes, and underpaid salaries.

Many are forced to focus on helping students, achieve good exam results rather than cultivating a deeper understanding of subjects. This shift toward exam-centric teaching leaves little room for creativity or personalized attention.

As a result, both teachers and students suffer, with the former feeling unfulfilled and the latter receiving a superficial education and still at the end the private schools make benefits.

Still as everyone isn't the same, there are teachers who really the teachers just like a catalyst for growth and some like the stifler of the growth.

A good teacher - A catalyst of growth

A good teacher is more than just an teacher, he is the mentor, teacher, guide, friend and a pure vessel of knowledge.

In our first chapter only, we discussed about how was the gurus(teachers) of that time and they still are there in some form, today.

Good teachers are like the ones who have the qualities such as patience, empathy, dedication, and a love for learning and teaching. They are the ones, who show the true path to students.

In the Gurukul system, teachers, known as gurus, would not just teach subjects; they would instill values, discipline, and life skills in their students.
They viewed education as holistic, nurturing the mind, body, and spirit of each students by focusing on each students unique personality.

In our modern classrooms, a good teacher continues this tradition by adapting their teaching style to meet the unique needs of each student. They recognize that not all students learn the same way or at the same pace, and they take the time to ensure that every student feels seen, heard, and supported.

A good teacher knows that their role is not just to impart information ,but is actually to ignite a passion for learning that students will carry throughout their lives.

Just take the example of Dr. APJ Abdul Kalam, India's former President and one of the greatest scientists.
Despite his many accomplishments, he remained deeply connected to his roots as a teacher.

He often shared stories of his experiences in the classroom, emphasizing that a good teacher is one who not only imparts knowledge but also instills values and a sense of purpose.

He spoke of his teachers with reverence, particularly one who sparked his love for science by encouraging him to think beyond textbooks and explore the world with curiosity.

Even when asked him you are a president, scientist, teacher and speaker, out of them which is the one personality in which you see yourself the most and is the most important for you, and despite being an president and scientist, his answer was of a teacher.

I want to even share a really good example of my one teacher, she is the one teaching me maths this year (2024-25)in 8th, she is also my class teacher this year, and she is just awesome.

Whenever you ask any student in the school about her, no one will complaint about her but would tell her the best teacher.

Like she is the one who never compare students or treat the students differently, but she is the one who always see every single student as the same in her eyes, use her unique teaching methods, and gives time to every single, especially the one like me who struggles in maths.

Also she teacher us moral science, and the lessons she gives about life, our just something that can shape anyone, who want to shape himself.

Similarly is my SST (social science) teacher of this year (24-25) , she is almost the same like my maths teacher , but the only difference is my maths teacher still scolds the students if they are non serious, but she(SST teacher) scolds no one and just treat everyone kindly and even because of this attention rate of the students increases, also she organize different activities of public speaking and debate in class so, that the students can explore themselves beyond textbooks.

A bad Teacher

While good teachers act as catalysts for growth, bad teachers, on the other hand, have a profoundly negative impact on a student's educational journey. The bad teacher is the one who sees teaching as merely a job, rather than a vocation or a calling.

Like today the explanation of most of the teachers is like this that if you will get good marks you will be respected in the eyes of teachers otherwise not. This is something that I see everyday.

Most of the teachers just have that "favorite" Students just because of that marks only.
But why? This was not same in the past, so why?

In the Gurukul system, a guru who failed to care for their student's holistic development would have been considered a poor teacher.

They would neglect the emotional or moral education of the student, focusing only on rote memorization of texts or a narrow subject focus, leaving the student without practical or ethical grounding.

In modern contexts, bad teachers often reflect similar shortcomings.

They teach with a rigid approach, focusing solely on completing the curriculum and preparing students for exams. Rather than nurturing a love for learning, they emphasize grades, competition, and conformity.

Rather than focusing on learning and growth, bad teachers also prioritize grades and marks which push the students into a competitive and stressful environment.
These teachers may also engage in unhealthy behaviors such as comparing students, fostering an environment of insecurity and pressure. They may unintentionally (or even intentionally) diminish a student's confidence by dismissing their questions or creativity.

A real-life example of how bad teaching can negatively impact a student can be found in Steve Jobs early school years. In various interviews, Jobs has mentioned how he struggled with school because he was bored by the rigid, test-focused environment.

His one of his teachers even labeled him as a troublemaker. Jobs later credited his success not to traditional schooling, but to the mentors and figures outside the classroom who encouraged him to think differently and pursue his passion for innovation.

Even I want to share an example of my one the teacher, who teaches us science, she is my teacher from class 6th and now currently I am in 8th.

As science is my favorite and I am really good at science, who always understand each concept of science and even talking about scoring marks then I always score full marks in it. As I am good at science, both practically and academically, she treats me very differently from other students, especially the one who are not good at it.

A student like me can still say she is a good teacher, but I am the one who understands the reality, the one who are not good at science, she literally makes their fun in front of the whole class, also she does discrimination between the students and all that you can expect from a bad teacher.

And there are my some friends who are not good at science, and they always come to me and take help in science, and always say, bro we never enjoy class and never able to understand, not because of that we are not good at it, but just because of the teacher.

Just even because of her, they start sometimes start prioritizing marks, that we want to also score good marks ones, and show her!
Without understanding the reall thing!

Also because of her they started hating such a wonderful subject, which is really sad.

Now there are teachers who say us that if you will study today and will be scoring good marks in future then only will be remembering you in our life.
Now tell me that was MS Dhoni, Sharukh Khan were the students who were scoring good marks?
No.

Now tell me will there teachers today will be not remembering them for their life?
Of course.

So why these teachers have that limiting beliefs only that the success is only by becoming a doctor or an engineer so that they will remember why?

Can a student excel in every subject?

As a student I have seen that every single teacher wants that every student should be good in my subject that is to the subject I am teaching.

Now tell is that possible for a student to be such except that "toppers" Who study for grades and marks?
No.

Even these teachers would not be the same.

Our several teachers say us that I was not good in this- that subject in school. So why they except something different from us?

Like my Hindi and Punjabi teachers always have the perception that I am not a good student or I don't score marks and so on.

This is just because I don't study both of these subjects and don't even enjoy in the class because of the lack of interest.

But do my Science, SST teachers or even my English teachers will have the same opinion about me as Punjabi and Hindi teachers?
No. Not at all.

Now if not me so do you know about one of the greatest mathematician of India - Srinivasa Ramanujan.

From a very early age only Ramanujan was a master of mathematics. His maths skills were such to a great extend that he was able to solve theories of university level in his early school life only.

He is even respected today by a millions just because of his great contributions in mathematics. He made substantial contributions to mathematical analysis, number theory, infinite series, and continued fractions, including solutions to mathematical problems then considered unsolvable.

Despite being a master of mathematics, in school he was the one who often fails in other subjects other than maths. And just because of this he was considered a failure by other teachers and even the school principals.
But the rest that we know is the history.

Exploitation of Teachers

The exploitation of teachers is one of the most under-discussed issues in education.

In many schools, especially in low-income regions, teachers are expected to work long hours for minimal pay by juggling multiple jobs just to make ends meet.

In some countries, the profession is underfunded, leaving teachers without the basic tools and resources they need to succeed.

Literally you also see around you, how many people are there who want to really become a teacher in future, teaching has become a profession which is just for the sack of a back up plan or something to support family by a little income and even because of this teachers really don't behave like teachers. Also they are the ones, who are not respected by the people and students around them.

Like a person works hard is whole life, by obtaining so called 'degrees' and a still at the end he doesn't gets that much which they deserve.

Every year private schools as we discussed, increase their fees, but the teachers still work on the same salary.Also they are over burned by the school work, as the private school doesn't hire people for specific tasks and force that tasks to be done by the teachers.

On the other hand, government teachers teaching in government schools, get the world class benefits without working much, they don't really focus on teaching because they get by doing less work also they are at the end getting their salary with increments.

Like,In India there was a teacher named Sangeeta kashyap. And Do you know, she has very interesting record with her. First let me tell who she was.
She was a teacher teaching in a government school of Indoor, India.
In 1990,she joined that school as a Biology teacher.

And now there is the record.

She has a record of being absent continually for 23 years. Yes, 23 years.

If you think that she is the only teacher like this, so let me tell you that according to a survey done by Kartik Murlidharan in 2010,in India there are 23.6% teachers who were announced during Unannounced school visits.
And this coated Indian government a loss of almost 1.5 billion that year.

And the best part is that, she was a teacher teaching in a government schools
Moreover, many teachers feel disempowered. They are asked to follow rigid curriculums and teach to standardized tests, reducing their role to that of an automaton delivering pre-determined content.

This not only stifles their passion but also prevents them from using their skills and creativity to truly impact students' lives. The lack of support and respect for teachers contributes to a system where educators are more likely to burn out or disengage

Ch 7 The murder of practical knowledge

I want to ask a question to all of you, can you replicate the same theoretical knowledge into the practical one by making a model or something to explain the theory?

I think so most of you will not be able to, or if then it would not be something really great or out of the box!

This is just because, In our today's education system, the focus on rote learning and textbook knowledge has increasingly led to the "murder" of practical and the real hands-on learning. You may also find it around you, where a student is able to tell the same thing theoretically, but not able to explain it or make it happen practically.

Like I see some students around me who are able to tell that on the exam sheet what exactly is the reason behind this is happening in science but when it comes to really explain it, they are blank.

One more example, I have seen students around me who top in English exams or other language subjects, but when it comes to speaking they always fumble or are not able to speak.

On the other hand, there are some who don't get good marks in that exam, but still when it comes to speaking, they are just blank.

So now just tell, should we respect a person getting more marks, or the one who is able to speak?

The Historical Roots

In past , the Gurukul system was one of the most respected forms of education which is something that we know.

In that, The gurus (teachers) imparted knowledge through interactive discussions, practical experiences, and by encouraging students to think critically because they were allowed to think out of the box and ask questions properly to the gurus without any hesitation.

At that time, There were no formal textbooks, and learning was not just about acquiring information but about how to live a meaningful and skillful life. Students learned by doing whether it was learning the art of war, agriculture, or medicine.

For instance, if a student wanted to learn archery, they would not sit in a classroom memorizing the parts of a bow and arrow.

Instead, they would practice archery under the direct supervision of their teacher.
And this us something that you also understood that, if a one wants to master himself in football, he has to really push himself,learn,train and come out of his box and practice in the field, as he can not master it by actually reading a book on it.

Similarly, The guru would provide continuous feedback, ensuring that the student not only understood the theory but could apply it in real-world situations. This method created a deep connection between knowledge and its practical application which nurtured students into capable, skilled individuals.

But today, we can see that when it comes to practical teaching, it is just like a myth.

This is because of one the reasons that are textbooks maybe, as where that textbooks should be a help tool for educators to teach, it has just became like a replacement of them.

Like even if you are having a book of let's say geography, you might understand 75% of the topic with just reading the topic from the book and even to understand totally(100%), today you have different things like Google and AI.

Where there is no problem with learning the theoretical part because of the internet, the problem is in the real life application, and that is something should be in the schools.

And also a problem is not like that we are studing from books today or there is something wrong in that like this also, the main problem is actually that even if I go to ask my parents, have you studied this same topic in your school?

They always answer 'yes'.

And then I always get a question in my mind why I am studying the same topic today when every single thing from that time to today is changed.

In contrast, the introduction of textbooks in modern schooling has shifted the focus away from hands-on learning.

The books replaced a significant portion of the teacher's role as the sole source of knowledge. While books can be incredibly beneficial for organizing information and allowing independent study but their dominance in classrooms has sidelined the practical aspect of learning.

The unfortunate consequence has been the replacement of the holistic approach with a rigid, exam-focused system, leading to a diminished emphasis on critical thinking and real-world skills.

Textbook VS Practical knowledge

Today, schools focus predominantly on what is written in textbooks. Education is largely measured by how well students perform in written exams, where answers must match the content in these books.

The problem with this system is that students are often learning to memorize information for exams without truly understanding the concepts or knowing how to apply them practically.
Can you even imagine that because of this all (memorizing and learning without understanding) , there was student who suffered from immense shame and Embracement in front of the audience of more than 600 people around him.

Like, Arjun was considered a very bright and intelligent student by his teachers in class 2. He always had a habit of memorizing facts from his textbooks and rarely made mistakes during exams. But his success was built on rote learning; he simply memorized everything without really understanding it.

One day, in class 6, his habit caught up with him.

During an orientation session, a speaker asked the students, "How many seasons are there in India?" Confidently, Arjun replied, "There are four seasons."
The hall went silent, and then a few giggles broke out. The speaker gently corrected him, explaining that India actually has six seasons: summer, winter, autumn, spring, monsoon, and pre-winter.

At that moment, Arjun felt embarrassed.

He realized that despite being seen as a smart student, his rote learning had left him with gaps in basic knowledge.

The incident changed how he saw his studies; he wasn't the same confident student anymore, and the experience made him question the effectiveness of memorizing facts without true understanding.

For example, students in science classes might study the theory of thermal electricity in detail. They might know the definitions, equations, and even the historical background of how thermal electricity was discovered. But when it comes to constructing a real thermal electricity model, many students would be at a loss.

They lack the practical experience to turn their theoretical knowledge into a working model. This disconnect is particularly troubling because, in fields like science and engineering, practical skills are essential.

The same issue arises in subjects like public speaking or debate.

Many students may read books about communication skills, memorize speeches, and even score well on written exams about the techniques of public speaking.

However, when faced with a real audience, many lack the confidence and skills to deliver their speech effectively. The absence of regular, hands-on practice robs students of the opportunity to develop competence in these areas.

The shift away from practical learning is not just limited to science or communication; it is pervasive across all subjects.

In economics, students memorize supply-and-demand graphs but rarely engage in real-life market analysis or entrepreneurial projects.

In history, students learn dates and events but are not encouraged to critically analyze historical sources or debate different interpretations of historical events.

In language classes, students memorize grammar rules but seldom engage in meaningful conversations or creative writing activities that would actually enhance their linguistic ability.

Is the Rise of Coaching Classes a New Form of Practical knowledge?

About the coaching classes and institutions, will further discuss in this
book, but for now we have understood a piece of it.

Like in recent years, the limitations of traditional schooling have given rise
to a parallel education system: coaching classes and private institutions.
These institutions cater to students who seek more specialized knowledge,
particularly for competitive exams.

While coaching centers claim to provide more targeted and effective
teaching than schools, they often fall into the same trap of focusing on exam
performance rather than true learning.

Now just because of this what happens is that , Many students no longer
feel the need to pay attention in school because they believe that their
coaching classes will provide all the knowledge they need to pass their
exams.

This is particularly true in countries like India, where students often attend
coaching centers for entrance exams like IIT-JEE, NEET, or CLAT. While
these institutions may provide valuable strategies for cracking competitive
exams, they, too, but they really contribute to the death of practical
knowledge by focusing on short-term memorization and test-taking
techniques.

Like this we also form a equation that there are 10 different ways out for us
to learn that theoretical knowledge with a better understanding, but there
is nothing for the real life practical knowledge.
Why it is ? , it's a big topic.

The consequences of rote learning

The lack of practical knowledge in today's education system has
far-reaching consequences.

Students who graduate with degrees but no real-world skills and then they
find it difficult to succeed in their careers.

Employers today increasingly emphasize the need for skills such as problem-solving, creativity, teamwork, and communication , all of which require practical experience.

However, many students are entering the workforce without these essential skills.

A great example of someone who broke free from rote learning is Jack Ma, the co-founder of Alibaba. Jack Ma, who struggled academically and failed university entrance exams multiple times, has often spoken out about the dangers of an education system that focuses solely on rote memorization.

In his youth, the Chinese education system placed a heavy emphasis on rote learning, which didn't align with his natural talents for creativity and communication.

He often recalls how his difficulties in school made him feel like a failure, as he was not able to keep up with rote-based learning methods.

However, it was his passion for English and his desire to connect with people that helped him break free from the constraints of traditional education.
He would practice English by giving tours to foreign visitors in exchange for lessons, something that wasn't part of his school curriculum but was a real-life, practical approach to learning.

When he eventually built Alibaba, he championed creativity, adaptability, and open-mindedness in his employees by rejecting the rigid structures that had failed him.

He emphasizes how learning should be about understanding concepts and applying them in real life, not just memorizing facts. Ma's rise from a poor student in a rote-learning system to a billionaire entrepreneur is a testament to the fact that success in the real world comes from curiosity, practical knowledge, and the ability to think outside the box—not from memorizing textbooks.

This is particularly evident in fields like engineering and medicine.

A study published by the National Employability Report in India found that more than 80% of Indian engineering graduates are unemployable because they lack the necessary skills.

These graduates may know engineering theory inside and out, but when it comes to solving real-world engineering problems, they are ill-equipped. This is a direct result of an education system that prioritizes textbook knowledge over practical application.

The Digital Era

Interestingly, while traditional schooling struggles with the lack of practical knowledge, the digital age has brought forth new ways for students to learn hands-on skills.

Platforms like YouTube have become popular resources for students seeking practical knowledge. Many students turn to YouTube tutorials to learn skills ranging from cooking and coding to woodworking and graphic design.

The Internet has, in some ways, become the new guru, offering students a chance to learn directly from experts and enthusiasts who share their practical expertise.

However, while the Internet offers vast opportunities for practical learning, it also highlights the failures of traditional education. If students have to rely on YouTube to gain the practical knowledge they should be getting in school, then the system is clearly broken.

Schools need to reclaim their role as providers of both theoretical and practical knowledge by incorporating hands-on projects, real-world problem-solving, and experiential learning into their curricula.

At the end,education must be about more than just passing exams; it must
be about preparing students to face the challenges of the real world with
confidence, creativity, and competence.

Unit 3 The Students Perspective
Chapter 8 The modern experience of students in this system

So, before moving on, I have a question for all of you, Do you experience some sort of similar education system today that was in the past known by us before British rule?

The answer is for sure No, and why even I am asking that.

But it's important to for us to understand this system with the better eyeballs and hearts of a student actually experiencing it.

In our today's world , where education should be a fun and the ultimate path to achieve goals for students, today its actually something the opposite of it because of our today's education system.

Today, students like me find themselves facing enormous pressure to excel in nearly every aspect of life, from academics and extracurriculars to early career decisions in their school life itself.

Just there in past, What was once a time for exploration and growth which today, now feels like an intense race to meet unrealistic expectations that are put on the students by this system and society, where performance often matters more than personal understanding or well-being of the students.

And now this is something that I need not to tell this to you about how this effecting us all at a big level, that we are listing thousands of life every year by suicide as students like me.

Recent reports like NCRB's ADSI 2021 show a rise in student suicides that over 13,000 students died by suicide in 2021, with a daily average exceeding 35 which was around and totally 12500 in 2020 .

This is something that is suffered by most of the students of India especially the ones who are middle class or have that one mentality (Finaincially).
In recent years even, several high-achieving individuals in India have also shared their experiences on the same.

The intense competition in coaching hubs like Kota, Rajasthan, which prepare students for the highly competitive engineering and medical entrance exams, has put immense pressure on young students which at the end is like that Kota now is also known as the suicide hub of India.

Stories have emerged from students who spent years away from their families in hostel settings, with relentless study schedules and a strong focus on standardized testing.

These students report feeling isolated and burnt out, and some have even faced mental health struggles such as anxiety and depression.

Many of them feel their personal interests and well-being are often neglected due to this singular focus on academic exellence.

For many students, academic achievement isn't just about learning, it's a make-or-break factor in determining their future. Exams, entrance tests, and grades create a high-stakes environment, where every score feels like a milestone that could shape their lives.

Teachers and parents, driven by well-meaning concerns about future success, encourage students to prioritize academic performance above all else.

Take Riya, for example, a high school student who spends hours each night revising material for exams.

Even when she doesn't understand a topic, she feels pressured to memorize it so she can earn the grades her school expects. Her hobbies, like drawing and playing the guitar, have taken a backseat.

For her, the question isn't "What do I enjoy?" but "How can I perform well enough to meet expectations?"

This lack of balance takes a toll by leaving her feeling exhausted and burnt out by a system focused on numbers over knowledge.

After all even there is question is it even worth it to teach the students that subjects in such a way ?
Because at the end if schools really have a intention to teach students how actually things are so; then is this the right method?
Not at all.

I have seen in my school, teachers always says us to underline this-that and say do this- that- so, but that all isn't that it is important for our learning or we can apply that in future, but just for the sake of exams. The system today just have one intention that is not to educate the students but to just train them for the exams and get good marks there. Then they also have a philosophy sometimes that 'marks doesn't matter' and so on, but is that really seen in this system and the attitude of the teachers and schools.

Now at the end again a question why the hell you should really study this shit in schools when you are not able to earn much money with it.

Literally college and University dropouts are earning in millions or even billions.

Step jobs a high school dropout.
Mark Zuckerberg dropout.
Mukesh ambani university dropout.
Influencers on social media you can see them.
And their money.

Pressure of extracurricular activities

Well this is a another thing to be discussed. A student like me might fit in these sort of things today and even like this by understanding it's importance more than academics, but not every other student. I have seen some students ,mostly the so called "toppers" that they don't take part in these activities or competition outside it, just that their academics might not get effected.

Just a question or a thing to understand, are that activities just time pass? If yes then there is a problem with you, because I am the person who has always learned better outside the class.

I am the one who always likes to take part in debate competitions, MUN's, science model competitions, other sports events, and in normal events in schools like in conduction (anchoring) and plays (drama).

I have seen myself learning better from these competitions than boring lectures in class.Sometimes ,there are lectures in class which are interesting and times where I feel it's also ok here in class , and the reason of such classes is that basically at that times I am learning something better than the usually classes like - wether it's a life lesson or something like hands on learning but this sort of times comes rarely and the classes are like that only(boring) and have that outdated things with no means.

If till now also you haven't understood something , then just imagine that student A has topped in his class academically and then there is a person B, who won a debate competition organised by any of the organization, institutions of the city and then this for sure that after winning in that he will get some recognition in his school or in his known ones.

Now which one sounds better? Person A or B?

Of course person B. Because you have understand the importance of hands on learning and the real life skills that will help you in life more than academics.
I am the person who always believes that "knowledge is power" But that's not same as it's is , because I believe 'The ability to apply the real knowledge that you have in real life is the real power'.

Today we learn everything that we should but by actually hearing or reading it to which also we even don't know how to apply in real life or at worst don't know were to apply that, rather than actually learning by doing.

Jack Ma the co-founder of Alibaba, focuses a lot on the need for practical, hands-on learning. In his view, the current academic system overemphasizes rote memorization and standardized testing which simply leave students ill-prepared for real-world challenges. He believes that schools should nurture creativity, resilience, and critical thinking skills which basically highlights that students should learn to be adaptable and innovative to meet the demands of the new AI-driven world.

His educational philosophy grew out of his own journey that he travelled across the years he was a student.

Having struggled with academic expectations and repeatedly failed entrance exams, he eventually graduated with a degree in English.

His approach to education—and, later, to building Alibaba—was rooted in his experiences as a teacher.

He realized that nurturing curiosity and perseverance was crucial for success.

He famously referred to himself as the company's "Chief Education Officer" and encouraged activities outside academics, like sports and arts, to develop well-rounded individuals.

He urges educational institutions to evolve, stating that schools should help students "become creative, constructive, innovative, and independent thinkers."
But do our schools do that? No.

Ch 9 Early career decisions

I have a question to all of you, how many times you have really changed your minds to become something like to pursue a career since your childhood?
A lot of times? Even more than 15-20 times?

And that's not something special to you or others but to all of us.

We all have changed our minds tons of times that what we want to become.

Weather we are in school or outside, we always want to shine bright and make our parents proud which is a dream of every child from young age , but our system comes in between and just act like a very-very strong barrier which stop our flow.

The journey of a student is often marked by a pivotal moment ; when they are asked to make a career decision in their life especially when they are just at the age white they should explore themselves.

For most, this decision is forced upon them far too early , sometimes as young as 9 or 10, even before they've had a chance to explore their interests, strengths, or the vast opportunities available.

In many parts of the world, particularly in our country ,students are pressured to choose careers from a limited set of options which are mostly engineering, doctor , law, or government services.

But do you think that there are only these 5 to 6 common options available in today's world to pursue this as a career? No.

Do you think that successful personalities today say the young minds to just become something like them at the age of 24 - 25 or 28?
 No.

The burden of Career Decisions

By the time students reach their mid-teens, they are expected to choose a specific stream or subject that aligns with a future profession where they can achieve their dream life and also can fulfill the dream of their parents. This system rarely accounts for their personal interests, talents, or the evolving nature of job markets, with the changing world.

This is something that becomes a major reason of the pressure upon students and they start worrying about future and the fear of becoming successful in that field.

A report by the National Career Service highlights that over 85% of Indian students feel pressured to pick a career by grade 10.

 Many of the students regret these decisions as they are often based on societal norms and parents expectations rather than their own genuine interests.

Talking about society then, when already a student is suffering from immense pressure inside him and where that student needs someone to actually make him feel better and get out of the bubble of bloody hell, the relatives and the society comes into the play and increase the pressure on the students by comparing him to other students, telling the stories of other students and asking him about his future career plans , do you think that a student will be able to handle it?
 No.

Even, The societal emphasis on a few "prestigious" careers, such as engineering, medicine, or law, places immense pressure on students.

Like even if a student wants to follow some different path for his future and wanted to become something in which he/she is interested, then also society comes into the play and kill it up.

Whereas the society can have a very big impact on lowering down the pressure on the student and showing him the real path and reality of life, they help in being inside an illusion of darkness.

Even, this creates a climate of fear where failure is equated with personal inadequacy.

Let's say you have two dishes in front of you one is the which you have heard of and second is the you have never heard of like take first as pizza and second as some local dish of another state or area. Think that a common man will choose which it is the one of what you have heard of and that is Pizza. Same phenomena can happen in anything, literally anything in the life.

That can even happen with the career option and the best part it happens! If you have heard of a career like Doctor or engineer and the second which you have not heard like Phycologist (just example) , you will choose Doctor or engineer because you have heard of that and not as a Phycologist .

The students are there who first have a limited time for thinking about their future then the other thing they have very less options in front of them as their choices, but do that is the reality where there are only some limited career options in the world?

Really?

So why we get a number of more than 10,000 different careers in the world after searching on internet?

The problem is with us, that we aren't familiar with the careers around the world.

Limited career options

Students often perceive only a handful of professions as viable career options due to the lack of exposure to unconventional fields.

Still after the vast advancements in technology, creative industries, and niche professions, limited career counseling prevents students from exploring options like game design, ethical hacking, wildlife photography, or digital marketing and many more.

A survey conducted by LinkedIn revealed that 75% of students in India were unaware of modern career paths like data science or UX/UI design , which are one of the most fastly growing fields of today.

Even I would like to ask you that you might listened about professions like Doctor, engineering, business, law, accountant, farming etc as these all are one of the most common professions in the world because of our fucking education system . But have you listened about environmentalist, Ornithologist, audio engineer, bee keeper, paleontologist etc. I think so most of you haven't.

But why we still don't want to become one of that?

Even after the explosion of new fields like AI, renewable energy, and digital marketing, the societal narrative remains outdated.

Parents and educators often push students toward careers that are "secure" or "prestigious." And this creates a domino effect: With even so many students pursuing the same professions, industries like engineering and medicine are oversupplied, leading to underemployment.

Careers in creative arts, emerging tech, or vocational trades remain unexplored, depriving industries of diverse talent.

Why don't we know about them as they also professions?

Why today also after the rapid advancement of AI and design, why we still don't talk about the hundreds of professions linked to them?

The biggest reason of this is that there are paths set for us in that common professions that doctor, engineering and so on and we don't have to figure what all the next steps we have to take.

Just because of this people are there after growing up in their mid 20's say that this wasn't the thing that I wanted to do. I am not getting that passion from inside. I am not able to earn much here. I am not happy and so on.

These all are the reasons of unawareness and that old mentality of society that we are not able to grow as human beings and as a common species.

Just because of these reasons only the *National Employability Report in India highlights that nearly 80% of engineering graduates are unemployable due to a mismatch between their skills and industry needs.*

Or in 2018 , the economic times published a article in which they clearly mentioned that out of 93,000 candidate applying for the job of poen in Uttar Pradesh , 3700 were there who were PhD holders.

A 2019 report by the India Skills Report found that only 47% of graduates were deemed employable by employers. The primary reason cited was the lack

*of relevant skills, including critical thinking, problem-solving, and technical
expertise.*

And at worst, *in 2000 only 35% people were unemployed but now in 2024 the
number has increased upto 65%, and this is unemployment.*

In other fields where people are needed but we aren't aware about them,
there people are needed at a large scale but the people aren't there , and at
places
where we have people at a very large scale too then we are not able to fulfill
it because of the lack of skills.

Now after all of this we might that this all the shit that our system is giving
today only effects we students(individuals) but that not the case, because at
a large if seen and in reality it effects the economy of the country as well as
the society. But how?

Here it is!
                        Economic and Social cost

The first of all cost to us as a society and as a economy is the lost of all the
lives because of the mental pressure of this system, as each year we lose
more than 1,00,000 , which for sure had some unique talents that can be
used in the society and in the economy.

Second, that even when students are still at good position in their job, they
feel that dissatisfaction and a feeling of quit from there jobs, due to which
they aren't able to focus on their work and after all there is a huge
productivity loss that cost us millions every single year.

Parents invest highly in their children's education and for that they
sometimes sell their land, mortgage other things and borrow money from
relatives which in today's time mostly goes as a waste as the children are
unable to finally crack that which their parents want .

Similarly, A flood of graduates in limited fields like engineering has led to underemployment and poor job satisfaction. For instance, engineering colleges in India produce over 1.5 million engineers annually, but many remain unemployed due to a lack of demand and primarily due to the lack of skills.

Literally, you can get shocked that 36% of the students who are graduating from IIT Bombay, are not getting jobs to do.

And, Out of every 4 MBA graduates only 1 has a job, out of every 5 engineering graduate only 1 has a job and out of every 10 graduate only 1 is employed.
What is this?

As former U.S. President Barack Obama once said, "We need to out-educate and out-innovate the rest of the world. That starts with giving every child the opportunity to learn, to dream big, and to achieve their full potential."

According to report by McKinsey, the demand for data scientists and AI experts is growing rapidly, but education systems are not keeping pace, leaving thousands of jobs unfilled.

This system is same and rigid, in which still we are only learning the old things which are something that can't be used today, and the worst part is even when AI and advanced tech is there , the syllabus is still same.

This is creating a big problem that students in school are just spending time just memorising that which will not be of any use in the future.

At last a problem which is somewhere hide in a mud bucket that is, we might be feeling that India is producing enough engineers even in terms of quantity which is somewhat fulfilling the needs of the country.
But No.

According to the All India Council for Technical Education (AICTE), around 60% of engineering graduates remain unemployed each year.

Why? Just because of this system.

Talking about doctors than India even after producing almost 90,000 MBBS graduates every year and having a better ratio in terms of doctors which is even

better than WHO standards, still India has a shortage of doctors, with a ratio of one doctor for every 1,450 people, which is below the World Health Organization's (WHO) recommended ratio of one doctor per 1,000 people.

Ch 10
The Reality of learning today

Gallup polls and surveys conduct a lot of surveys on how a average man think that want is education? And what is the use of it or it can do to you? It shows that many people view education as the foundation for personal and professional success.

They believe it provides the knowledge, skills, and critical thinking abilities necessary to thrive in today's complex world.

But do you think that the education served today in front us in our schools our actually building our knowledge, skills and critical thinking?

Their might be some who would directly say 'no' and it is also true, but there might be some think that my statement is wrong.

Basically they really believe that education really provides knowledge, skills and critical thinking abilities.

Now I want to ask them again in which century they are currently living? And how much time they on average spend in their schools and then at tuitions?
The answer is simple in 21st century. And we on average spend our 5-6 hours in schools and then 1-2 hours at tuitions.

Now again ask yourself is that worth it to spend this much time, money and energy on this sort of education in such a system with such a way of teaching, where you have access to AI, YouTube, google, internet, WiFi etc.

Really talking about me, then I am currently in class 8 and I have always understood my concepts better from mobile rather then in schools, where at my home only I can learn and understand better , save my time and energy and also money, which I can invest in other things for my personal growth.

Talking about these all the things like AI(chat gpt) , YouTube, google and internet & WiFi, we always talk about their side effects today in 2024 , but for students it is something more than a boon.

If a person wants to really utilize something in a better way and learn something then a person like me can even learn from watching movies where I make notes of the movies from which I have really understood and learned something new for my growth.

I always have stuff in my mobile which is valuable for me at a big level and I have really learned better and more from mobile than in my class.
For example I have never learned any of the public speaking skill or this book writing skill from my school but from my mobile by utilising it in a write way.

For even understanding my one topic of class 7th better I just wrote about the phenomenon of sea breeze and land breeze , then I just watched a simple short video of a channel of "science with fun" and I understood the topic just from than simple 1 minute video, which literally took us 30 minutes in class to understand just one single topic.

Then what we are doing?

Where schools can be a place where we can learn to actually implement the theories into the real life in basic manner where in collages we can advance it, "We are just learning how to exell in exams".

That too we are learning to exell in exams by rote memorization and standardized testing instead of actually understanding the meaning of the concept.

Actually the schools should focus on practical knowledge and the implementations of the theories in real life.

A study by FICCI and NASSCOM in 2020 highlighted that over 60% of academic courses in Indian universities were outdated and did not align with industry requirements.

A student like me who always uses AI and YouTube for understanding the concepts better or use it as a modern source of tuition classes, understand far more better from it, and I really think so that in class I just waste my time understanding that concept.

The reality of learning today is worst till such an extend, like in the time of AI, internet, softwares and data science, in my computer science classes we are still learning that MS PowerPoint, MS excell and all.

That too where we have AI applications to use in it, we are still using it manually.

Like this is also a thing that I don't understand, whenever the summer vacations or winter break comes, our schools start giving us the work from all over the world and that all are something related to that practical knowledge only- making models, projects etc.

These all the things are not something that are taught to us actually in the schools , but we all actually make that too by using YouTube and AI.
So what is the use of these schools?

My motive of going to school is clear that is networking, fun with friends, extra circular activities like debate competitions, MUN's, anchoring, dramas, science exhibitions ,etc , but the actual reason because of which my parents are sending me to school that isn't cleared by the school at all.

Even what are schools really teaching in the classes - rubbish that is of new use.
There are some basic things in life like how to write a email, or about critical thinking,how the tax system works, to speak effectively, and many more.
But these basic things are not only in this system.

The world is changing every day but the system is same and the topics to learn are same.

This system destroys the crucial and important 10 years of our life, which can be fully utilized in a better way to learn life skills and a lot.

Ch 11 The Role of coaching classes and institutions

How many of you go to any sort of coaching classes, institutions or tuitions
after your school to repeat the same topics there that were in school?
I think many of you.

Now, I want to ask you, how many of you go to these places for the same of
really understanding the concept that you didn't understood in the school?
How many of you go for the same of more marks?

How many of you go because your parents have hanged you at that places?
How many of really want to go there?

Well the answers might be whatever, but one question remains the same,
Do the schools really worth it after all of this just for the purpose that are
parents are sending us to schools?

Well; let's see
To first understand the reality of these institutions, we have to first study
the history of it.

The Rise of Coaching institutions

The coaching institutions that we see today started gaining recognition in
the mid 20th century.

Initially, these were small-scale setups which were led by passionate
educators who offered supplementary classes to help students struggling
with specific subjects especially maths and science.

The primary aim of this was to provide additional support beyond the
traditional school curriculum.

In India, the idea of coaching centers gained traction in the 1960s and
1970s, particularly for prestigious examinations such as the JEE and UPSC
entrance exams.

The establishment of IITs in the 1950s created a high demand for structured preparation, and coaching institutes became the go-to option for students aiming to secure admission.

Till the time it was serving this purpose it was still okay if they were really doing so, but as the late 20th century started, this changed the purpose of these institutions.

Even though these were specifically started by the passionate educators, they started emerging at a very small level on the society to which we today know as tuitions .

The late 20th century saw a significant transformation as coaching evolved from personalized tutoring to commercial enterprises.

Kota, in Rajasthan, India, has become synonymous with the coaching industry and is often referred to as the "coaching capital" of the country.

This city is home to around 150 coaching institutes, including prominent names like Allen, Bansal Classes, and Resonance.

These institutes primarily prepare students for competitive exams such as the IIT-JEE and NEET.
Over the years, Kota's coaching ecosystem has evolved into an estimated ₹800 crore market, with an annual growth potential of 15%.

Historically, Kota's rise began in the 1980s with the establishment of Bansal Classes, which successfully guided students to top engineering institutions. This success attracted more institutions which turned Kota into a hub for competitive exam preparation.

The city now attracts approximately 100,000 students annually from across India, making it a central player in the national coaching market.

Globally, the private tutoring industry, which includes such coaching hubs, which grow at 15-20% annually, and is driven by a competitive education system and the demand for specialized test preparation.

Coaching institutions have transitioned from being supportive aids to dominant players in education, shaping careers but also raising questions about the true purpose of learning.

Now the main point, if these sort of things were only for the students who have passed 10th still it was fine, though it also has the same history like school which started from knowledge centres but today have become a commercial houses.

For the students below 10th standard, going to these institutions and tuitions ; here the main story comes.

For many students, life becomes a juggling act between school and coaching classes.

This dual system of education often leaves them physically and mentally drained.

A typical day for these students starts early in the morning at school and ends late at night with coaching classes which leaves a very little time for relaxation, hobbies, or family.

Like I don't go to any coaching class after my school, but I see my friends going to school, coming back to home and then again going to tuitions to repeat the same things there at tuition.

The students who are not in class 10th and when they are going to tuitions, a question takes birth are these coaching classes better than these schools in terms of that academics , and I think so they are to some extend.

A student like me who don't goes to any of these coaching classes, but still performs better than 90% of the students in terms of academics, I also take help of internet as a substitute to coaching classes because in schools there is nothing in terms of that too.

For me going to school and fucking my life there has only 3 reasons: first, is networking, meeting new people through extra activities, outside class or school and enjoying with friends Second, taking part in extra activities like debate, MUN's ,science competitions , functions or events in schools etc. Third, because my parents are sending me there.

Other than these reasons there is not even a single reason that I go to school.
The reasons that I told you, the coaching classes don't have this, but the reason are parents are sending us to school is somewhat better in that classes.
So, is that worth it to spend so much on that schools plus on the coaching classes where you can get the same useless knowledge in a better way on internet in a better useful way?

Coaching centers are undeniably effective in preparing students for exams.

Their focused curriculum, rigorous training, and frequent testing equip students with the skills needed to perform well still under the exam conditions, but a very big problem that occurs is that these institutions put the emphasize on following things like ; Cramming Over Understanding - The primary goal of coaching centers is to ensure high scores. As a result, they prioritize rote memorization over conceptual understanding, leaving students ill-equipped for practical applications.

And neglect of Holistic Development like Coaching centers rarely focus on soft skills, emotional intelligence, or creativity like essential attributes for success in life.

Or Questionable Ethics- Some institutes employ high-pressure tactics, misleading advertisements, and even resort to unfair practices to attract students and maintain their reputation.

The rise of coaching centers raises uncomfortable questions about the role and effectiveness of schools.

Ideally, schools should provide a comprehensive education that prepares students not just for exams, but for life. However, the reality is far from this ideal.

If coaching centers are stepping in to fill the gaps left by schools, one must question why parents and students are paying twice ; once for school and again for coaching.
Both the places in terms of "academics" are just ruining students life.

There are students who want to do something big and better in some other field of life, but they get stuck here in this piece of shit.
And , After all of this in between whose life is getting destroyed?
Students.

Where they are not able to get time for themselves, not able to learn skills needed in today's world, wasting their time of useless stuff,not able to explore,being burn out etc.
Even parents and families suffer from some of the problem due to this dual edge. How?

Like it leaves a big financial Strain on Families and creates a toxic environment for students filled with pressure, which is also transferred to the parents in some sort of ways.

At the end, This rise of coaching institutions highlights the failures of mainstream education.

While they serve a purpose, their existence underscores the urgent need to reform the school system. Until schools become centers of holistic learning, the parallel system of coaching centers will continue to dominate, leaving students overburdened, families overcharged, and society shortchanged.

The question remains the same that Can we break this cycle and create an education system that truly serves its purpose?

Unit 4 The Role of Parents
Ch 12 Parenting and education

Parents.
They are the most important part of a child's life.

A child like me has nothing above than his parents for him and I am sure I
am not the only one .

They are the first teachers, friends and everything of a child.
In this unit we have to cover the role of parents in students education
journey, how they effect it.

Parents play a very crucial role in shaping their child's educational journey
who often acts as the first teachers and the most significant influencers in
their child's life.

While schools and governments design curricula and policies, parents are
the bridge between these systems and their children's unique needs.
From providing emotional and moral support which helps children
navigate life's challenges.
To instilling values, ethics, and cultural beliefs which at the end shapes the
child's character.

The role of parents in education

How many of you go to schools because you wanted to go to school when
you were a child?
Anyone?
I think there might be very few in number.

Such was a case with Albert Einstein.

Him? Really?

Yes! We see lives without the struggle and the story behind it, that why some you can be shocked.

Albert Einstein as known is one of history's greatest minds who struggled significantly during his early education due to the choices made by his parents.
They enrolled him in the Luitpold Gymnasium, a traditional German school focused on rote memorization and strict discipline. However, Einstein's creative and inquisitive nature clashed with the rigid teaching methods.

At school, Einstein was labeled a "poor student" and was often stopped for questioning established norms. Teachers dismissed him as unremarkable, famously saying, "You will never do anything."

His parents, believing in the school's reputation, pushed him to conform while being unaware of the toll it was taking on his mental health and confidence.

Eventually, Einstein's unhappiness became evident, and his parents withdrew him from the school.

They sent him to the Aarau Cantonal School in Switzerland, which put a heavy stress on creativity, critical thinking, and conceptual understanding. In this progressive environment, Einstein thrived, laying the foundation for his revolutionary contributions to science.

His story highlights the importance of tailoring education to a child's unique needs. His life stands as a testament to how the wrong educational decisions can stifle talent, and the right ones can unleash brilliance.

Even after putting him in that "creative" school we already know what happened then.

Sending a child to school and wasting his crucial and the most important 12 years of his life is on of the worst decisions that the parents make.

Just because now it has become a ritual, everyone follows it blindly and get stuck in a paradox.

If we say that parents are just ruining the lives of thier children by sending them to school then it can make you to think more and more. But interestingly in United States of America, there are more than 5 million children who don't go to school, not because they can't afford it, but because there parents are not sending them to school because they know the reality of this system.

But now comes the best part, out of that 5 million students , more than 75% student's parents are teachers. Really!

The teachers also know that what the hell is this system.

Now these all were about sending the child to school.
But now comes the most important part.
The effects of parents in their child's educational journey.
Have you seen your parents telling you that if you will score these much marks, get this much of percentage, you will get this.

Now, when you see this with a naked eye ball then it seems fine to you, like parents are basically creating a feeling inside the children to study in the greed of that 'something'.

But if you will now go inside it and look through a lens then you will find that parents here are simply telling the students to get these much of marks by whatever way and you will get this.

Here marks are created as the end goal to get that 'something' , but in this process - greed, the children simply keeps the learning aside and just focus on getting that much marks that they can get that thing that they want.
Now is it good?

No. Not at all.

And have you seen some parents focusing on their child but creating a very restricted parenting approach?

Parents that lie under this category focus heavily on formal education from the very beginning. They emphasize structured learning, often introducing academic concepts like reading, writing, and math as early as possible. And this is something that most of the parents in our country do.

Like how they introduce any of the concepts to their child?

Formalized Methods like use of books, flashcards, and workbooks to teach numbers, alphabets, or science early on from the starting itself instead of really teaching at only at their own in an interesting way.

Also they are Routine-Oriented means there are strict schedules for learning, with less time for free play or exploration.

Like an example : A parent might insist their child learn multiplication table of 3 at the age of 4 .

Now this is something that leaves no room for imagination or unstructured play.
Now what this actually does?

 This make that child a quick learner but risks that are turning the child into a rote learner and having always a cramb mentality. Because they don't teach the child in a really interesting manner but by just making that child recalling the table of 3 again and again and like this a series, a poem in that child's mind and to this our Indian parents say learning.

I have told you in the starting of this book too, that we all even our parents are the part of this education system and to change this we have to change every single out of it.

Now on the other hand, there are some parents that use a different approach to teach their children from the starting itself because they have a different mentality.

These parents prioritize curiosity, creativity, and a love for learning over formal academic achievements or that 'rote learning'. They introduce concepts informally, often through play and observation.
How They Introduce Concepts?

By play-based learning like , Teaching numbers through games, alphabets through storytelling, or science through everyday activities like gardening. Experiential Approach like , Encouraging questions like "Why does the sun rise?" or "How do plants grow?" to spark natural curiosity.

And Flexibility by allowing the child to learn at their own pace without rigid academic goals.

This type of knowledge is the one which has long lasting effects on the students.
Like, Builds a lifelong love for learning and problem-solving.

Fosters creativity and critical thinking.
Develops emotional intelligence and adaptability and many more.
Now just tell me which is the better method and has the best outcomes?
Of course the second one.

But we are always taught with the first method and that causes us in the worst way it can.
By this I just want to tell you about how parents are also the one who have a very big influence in this education system.

Parents are the one that from the starting itself can kill a child's curiousity .

Most of the parents, under societal pressure, prestigious positions and the burden of competition, prioritize rote learning and results over creativity and
exploration.

In doing so, they unintentionally suppress a child's natural curiosity and his self believes which are the real powers that the students have and will make him achieve his goals.

Some of the common ways of the same are which I think so every single student especially in India experiences.

The first and the main one is over emphasis on grades and marks by some of the common methods.

Now to solve this we have to bring a shift in Conversations like, Instead of engaging in discussions about what their child is curious about, parents ask questions like, "What was your rank in class?" or "How much did Sharma's son score?"

Even if their child might have scored 85/100 they might be happy till the time they get to know that Sharma's son has scored 90/100.

This is something that has not happened with me but with my friends because of me.

Like they are the one getting scolded here , and I becomes that "Sharma's son".
This results in only pressure to perform. Parents compare their child's grades with others, equating higher scores with better future prospects.

This simply creates an immense pressure on the child to perform, regardless of their interest or understanding of the ssubject

Also something that has happened with me is like even of I studied for an hour, my mother still tells me to study more and only get that "good marks".

For me that is like if I have studied for that 1 hour , that is just to satisfy my parents that I am studying and getting good marks but really I don't have any of the interest in these textbooks than even in science.

Only thing for me is important in these academics is to ask questions and question in the class, take part in activities and so on.

This is something that is not in the report cards that is why this is the situation with me. But still I am all far than this because, every single teacher of mine just praises me and treat me as their favorite student in the class and this is something that my parents know about.

Just because of this, there is a loss of Genuine Interest in Learning of the students.

Children begin to study for marks, not for knowledge. They memorize facts instead of understanding concepts, killing their innate curiosity.

Some of the other part is that when children constantly ask "why," they are not merely being inquisitive , they are trying to understand the world.

However, parents and teachers , often unintentionally, shut down this curiosity with phrases like, "Because I said so" or "Stop asking silly questions."

While this may seem like an innocent or necessary response in the moment, over time, it significantly impact a child's mindset, creativity, and confidence.
This is something that is very common with me, because I like to question every single bit of anything, my parents and teachers just say silently " Raghav; This is like this only for now just focus on this then other things".

This is all because of the system itself, like asking questions in this system is a sign of disrespect or half of the times parents and teachers don't know the answer of it.

Even Thomas Edison was an exceptionally curious child who always had the habit of annoying his teachers and parents with endless questions about how things worked.

While his teachers considered him "difficult," his mother encouraged his curiosity and even took him out of school to teach him at home. This nurturing environment allowed Edison to become one of history's greatest inventors.

Now just a short lesson of this is : If his mother had dismissed his questions as "silly," the world might never have seen the electric bulb.

Now just think for a while the parents who encourage curiosity at every single turn.

They recognize that curiosity is the foundation of innovation and success.

Now there are numerous Ways Parents Encourage can Curiosity like Asking Open-Ended Questions; Instead of giving answers, they ask, "What do you think?" to promote critical thinking.

Supporting Passions; These parents encourage children to explore their interests, whether in science, arts, music, or sports.

Focusing on Learning, Not Marks; They celebrate effort and the process of learning, not just grades.

Allowing Mistakes; Mistakes are seen as opportunities to learn rather than failures.

Do you know that this all that I told in the above text was a reality of someone's home, to whome we today know as "Bill gates"

Ch 13 Under parenting VS Over parenting

Till the time we were discussing that all about parenting was on a normal pace of parenting, but now comes the part when parents are not even caring about what their child is doing.

This is common in the families that are often too rich or too poor where they don't have either the time or they don't care what their child is doing. This is something referred to as under parenting.

To understand this more I have a story to share with you all.

This story is of a boy to whom I know since class 3. He is the one who is famous in the whole school just because of his behavior and habits.

Like what can you expect at the very worst from a student of today's age who has access to mobile from a very early age, what can you expect from him?
He abuses teachers and others in front of all, he talks as much as bad about a girl he can.

He speaks as much rubbish you think he can. He fights and only stays out of the class. His dirty reactions and actions. His behavior. All are at the extreme levels.

Even after failing in every exam, not doing anything except wasting money, also after getting suspended thrice every month and more still his parents don't even give a damn to what he is doing.

They don't say him anything. But they still support him.
After all of this the words of his parents are like do whatever you want.
If you will fail in exams will get a activa and if pass will get a bullet/bike.
This is under parenting.

If want to understand in a more easy way then Under-parenting basically refers to a lack of adequate involvement, guidance, or nurturing in a child's life by his/her parents.

It can develop from various factors like external circumstances, personal limitations, or societal influences.

This is often seen in families where both the parents of the child are working and there is a very less time with them(parents) to spend with their child or there are the digital distractions that erode the quality family time, finiancial stress or dispute between parents are some of the common reasons of the same.

Now this under parenting has numerous effects on the students which almost shake the life of the child.

For eg even in the movies we have seen that if a villain has become a villain there was some role that parents have played by that " under parenting". The effects are vast like, Children may feel neglected, unimportant, or unloved.

They lack emotional and moral guidance, which leads to insecurity and poor decision making.

Children might grow up without proper emotional regulation by struggling with their own mental health issues.

They may feel unsupported or develop resentment toward their parents. And a lot.

So while not more than if this under parenting is a problem than just the opposite of it is over parenting.

Which is also not so wonderful but causes the same problems.

Over Parenting

Christopher Logan who is known as one of the smartest people in the world with an IQ of 195 grew up in a very troubled family.

But still like under parenting, this story sheds light on the just the opposite of it , what happens when there's over-parenting later on.

Langan's mother, after realizing his extraordinary intelligence, began to enforce extremely high standards by pushing him to excel academically and socially at an very early age.

His mother's excessive control on his life led to feelings of isolation and a sense of stress inside him.

Despite he was a genius, he lacked essential social and emotional skills because his upbringing was overly academic and devoid of emotional warmth.
He as the result rejected formal systems, struggled with authority, and chose to live a reclusive life.

If not in a difficult language then in simple terms, Over-parenting, or "helicopter parenting," refers to an overprotective and over-involved approach where parents excessively control or micromanage their child's life.

This behavior devlop from various psychological, societal, and cultural factors. While it may come from a place of love, it simply leads to unintended negative consequences.

The main cause of this over parenting is basically that the parents are to binded with their children and they express their love and feelings in such a way that not helps the child but actually causes problems for him.

Parents often project their fears onto their children by worrying about the child's ability to succeed in a competitive world.

The fear that a child might fail academically, socially, or professionally drives parents to micromanage every decision.

They feel the need to shield their child from failure at all costs.
As a result , Children miss out on valuable learning experiences gained through failure.

They may develop low self-esteem, as they feel incapable of handling challenges independently.

Now, Some parents strive for their child to be "perfect" in every way like academically, socially, and emotionally.

This comes from societal pressures, comparison with other parents, or personal insecurities.

They believe their child's success reflects their parenting skills.

Now this is something that this creates a immense pressure on the child which leades to anxiety and stress.

The child may become overly dependent on external validation and struggle with self-acceptance.

As we are living in the 21st century so just to take care and monitor every step of their child, they restrict independence out of fear of accidents, poor decisions, or negative influences.

Now this is just because of the love and fear, but how this results, like in the child's ability to develop decision-making and problem-solving skills.
The child might rebel against these restrictions in adolescence.

Some of the other things that are like the parents provide with every single resource to their child and now this makes them self depended on the parents and they as a result are not able to take the decisions on their own.

Ch 14 Providing Emotional Support and Creating a learning environment

We all know about Elon Musk but we don't know about the hands behind his success.

Behind his success, a very big role in his success is played by his mother.

His journey to becoming one of the world's most innovative entrepreneurs is deeply connected with the support and sacrifices of his mother - Maye Musk.
As a single mother raising three children,She faced countless challenges but still, her unwavering determination and belief in her children's potential never wavered.

She wasn't just a provider; she was a nurturer, a mentor, and the backbone of Elon's early life.

From a young age itself Elon Musk showed an insatiable curiosity about the world.

Instead of stifling his endless questions, Maye encouraged him to explore, to read, and to dream without limits.

She filled their home with books and fostered an environment where imagination and inquiry were celebrated. Whether Elon was lost in a science fiction novel or teaching himself programming on a computer he saved up to buy, Maye stood by him, often marveling at his ability to immerse himself in learning.

Life wasn't easy for Maye.
She juggled multiple jobs as a dietitian and model to make ends meet by working long hours just to ensure her children had access to the resources they needed.

Even when finances were tight and they were short of money still Maye prioritized opportunities for her kids to learn and grow. She encouraged

independence, teaching them to face adversity head-on, a lesson Elon carried into his adult life.

Elon's school years weren't without challenges. He was often bullied and felt like an outsider, but Maye was his constant source of emotional support.

She would remind him that being different was a strength and that his ideas, no matter how unconventional, had value.

When Elon faced failure later in life, such as the early struggles with Tesla and SpaceX, it was this resilience instilled by his mother that helped him persevere.

Maye's parenting was about giving him the tools and confidence to carve his own.

When he decided to pursue his wild dreams of colonizing Mars and revolutionizing the automotive industry, she didn't question him. Instead, she stood by him, offering encouragement while the world doubted his ambitions.
Like this we should know the importance of emotional support and creating a learning environment by the parents around a student is a very big deal onto success.

Parents have a crucial role in creating a balance where their children feel safe, supported, and inspired to explore their potential.

Now even after reading the story of Elon Musk, if you are still not sure that what is the importance of emotional support to the children by parents, then let's get it out.

Emotional support ensures that the child feel valued and secure in his life. This is essential for their mental well-being and academic success.

A child who is emotionally supported can tackle challenges, recover from setbacks, and pursue their goals with confidence and dedication to become the best version of his own self.

Now if we really know that how important is with providing the emotional support to the child, then how really can parents provide it.

The first and one of the most important is being present and attentive, like by spending quality time with the child and actively listening to their thoughts and concerns.

Also by acknowledging their emotions and validate their feelings instead of dismissing them.

Then the other one that is by encouraging open communication that is creating a judgment-free zone where children can share their fears, dreams, and failures.
Use empathetic language, such as, "I understand how you feel," to build trust.
The third one by Celebrating efforts over results.

And the last one can be setting real life expectations.

Now these all the things will literally be a wonder in child's life like it will improve their confidence, open their imagination , will build a better mental health and will build a strong relationship between the parents and the child.

After providing the emotional support to the child, the parents should now focus on creating a positive learning environment which will bring wonders in child's life.

When parents actively foster a culture of learning, children are more likely to develop critical thinking, problem-solving, and independent learning skills.
Now how to this?

Simply dedicate a learning space to the child.

Encourage curiosity , and incoprate real life learnings.

Providing emotional support and creating a learning environment are intertwined responsibilities that shape a child's academic and personal growth.

Parents who actively engage in these aspects empower their children to become resilient, curious, and independent learners.

By balancing guidance with independence, parents can help their children navigate the complexities of education and emerge as confident, capable individuals.

This approach not only enhances individual success but also fosters a culture of lifelong learning, benefiting society as a whole.

Do really parents do it?

Do parents really do this to their child?

Not at all.

The problem again comes to this education system only which have trained and made parents for that, because we know that every single parent in the world wants their child to be successful.

They have also gone through the same phase and being in this phase has made them this; and the rest of the role is that society plays off.

Unit 5 Rat Race/Matrix
Ch 15 What the hell is Rat Race?

I am sure that you might have listened this term (Rat Race) , as it has also become like a buzz word in today's time.

You might have seen Robert kiyosaki, Elon Musk and other business personalities and influencers talking about the same and also that the education system is the biggest and main cause of it.

So let's just understand first what exactly it is.
The "rat race" which is also known as matrix is an exhausting and a meaningless cycle of competition, where people chase after societal standards of success like marks in school , degrees, or even money without ever feeling fulfilled.

It is just like running on a treadmill which is always and always moving but never truly getting anywhere.

This term as though modern in usage, has roots in the pressures of industrialized societies, where people were expected to work tirelessly, at the cost of their personal lives and passions.

This trap is there to kill you from inside, and most of the people around you are in this trap only.

You must have listened that 'life is a race', run fast in life and so on ; what it is? Rat Race.

And I am also sure that you might have listen this from your teachers or parents, who are in the same trap and want you to fall in this.

Exactly they don't want you to fail, because for them it's like success but in actual it's nothing.

Think about it just that like from a young age itself, students are pushed to achieve high grades, get into prestigious colleges, and secure high-paying jobs here the focus is not on learning, growth, or individuality but on ticking off boxes that society considers "successful."

This system, reinforced by rigid curriculums and societal expectations, conditions people to fit into predefined roles.

The result? A loss of individuality.

People end up following the same script.

They rarely question whether their goals are truly their own. This loop doesn't just trap them but shapes entire systems - our schools, workplaces, and even families - that prioritize conformity over creativity, passion, and genuine fulfillment.

This rat race isn't just about running; it's about running in the wrong direction which is driven by a fear of falling behind rather than a pursuit of what truly matters.

Breaking free from this means stepping back, questioning these norms, and daring to live on your terms , not society's.

Now further in this unit will talk about how this system make you fall in this trap, how it causes you and how you can actually get out of it.

Ch 16 The system training you for this trap

In the starting of the book only we have discussed about how this system changed from wisdom oriented to a factory and then a large business model.
Just how this system is made and the working of this system is enough to make you fall into this.

Still learning the old things that will be of no use in the future, the old curriculum, standardized teaching methods and competition, chase of marks and all of this is enough to make you a rat.

Now, Rather than exploring your passions or developing problem-solving skills, students are often conditioned to chase metrics of success like grades, rankings, and degrees that are increasingly disconnected from real-world needs and most importantly they are of no use in the future.

According to a 2018 World Economic Forum report, nearly 65% of children entering primary school today will eventually work in jobs that don't yet exist or will not exist in the future.

Yet, schools largely ignore teaching skills like adaptability, emotional intelligence, and financial literacy the skills critical for thriving in a rapidly evolving world.

Instead, the curriculum is often decades old, teaching subjects in isolation and failing to address modern challenges like managing finances, understanding taxes, or developing interpersonal skills.

The students today don't even know basic things like writing an email which is still ok now because of the AI and Internet, but just like that only while having AI and Internet with us we are still learning the things of no use in future, instead of some valuable stuff , why so?

The chase of marks and pressure to academic success, just makes them a puppet or a rat running on a never ever stopping treadmill

But how do you actually fall into this trap?

The rat race begins early in life, often without individuals even realising it. From childhood itself societal norms push students toward conventional "secure" career paths.

Parents, teachers, and peers unknowingly reinforce this cycle by equating in academic performance with self-worth and future success.

While these pressures may be well-intentioned, they simply lead students to prioritize stability over innovation, choosing safe but uninspired careers that offer little personal fulfillment.

As these students grow, financial problems like student loans, societal expectations, and the fear of failure tighten the noose.

The cycle is just like this that they study in school, they graduate, secure a job, and begin climbing the corporate ladder, without stopping to question if their chosen path aligns with their true aspirations.

As earlier in the book we discussed about how we students still know about career path such as doctor and engineering but not zoology and geologists.

Now as the path to medicine and engineering is already made in front of our eyes , with also the rent-less pressure of society, we all just walk in the heard mentality, become a mediocre one, and just follow that secure job path and just fall into this matrix.

Then whole life, people think, "Why did I do this and not that?"

We all also read the stories and listen of people who actually are something today, and why they are there that they are the top 5% ?

Just because they broke the cycle and trap of Rat Race.
People like Elon Musk, Bill gates, Shahrukh Khan, Christiano Ronaldo, actually didn't follow that mediocre paths and tried something extraordinary to actually become that extraordinary.

A Way Forward

A way forward you can actually think of is Life is not a race; it is actually a journey of exploration and growth.

The sooner we stop treating it as a competition, the freer individuals will feel to forge their unique paths.

True success lies not in conforming to societal expectations but in pursuing a life of purpose, passion, and fulfillment.

The rat race may seem all-encompassing, but with awareness, courage, and a shift in perspective, it is possible to step off the treadmill and design a life that is truly your own.

The rat race isn't just a system - it's a mindset.

Life is not a Race

The notion that life is a competition , a relentless chase to outperform others has become deeply embedded in the modern culture of today.

From school rankings to career ladders, the structure of society condition individuals to view success as a finite resource by simply creating an endless loop of comparison and rivalry.

But; *life is far more complex and meaningful than a mere race to which actually this education system actually makes.*

Philosophically, life should be about finding purpose, experiencing growth, and achieving fulfillment.

Albert Einstein once said, "Everybody is a genius.

But if you judge a fish by its ability to climb a tree, it will live its whole life believing that it is stupid." This quote is discussed by us earlier in book too, that simple tells about the unique personalities that one have.

As in the starting of the book too, I explained how this system understands that you are someone opposite of that fish, but no we are actually like that fish only.

True success lies not in outrunning others but in understanding oneself and contributing meaningfully to the world, or it is about achieving your true goal and making your parents proud of you.

Even Simon Sinek, a prominent author and speaker, emphasizes this in his book - "infinite game."

According to Sinek, life is not about winning or losing but about staying in the game, constantly learning, and aligning actions with personal values.

Success, in this context, becomes a deeply individual journey rather than a collective comparison.

The race metaphor leads to burnout, stress, and dissatisfaction.

It creates a mindset where individuals are constantly chasing external validations like wealth, fame, or status while neglecting internal growth and happiness.

Instead of racing through life, a more fulfilling approach involves embracing the process, learning from experiences, and nurturing relationships and passions.

Life is not about how fast you move or how far you get compared to others. It is about the depth of your journey, the lives you touch, and the legacy you leave behind.

Breaking free from the race mindset requires courage to define success on your own terms and the wisdom to see life as an evolving journey, not a finite competition.

So, how this Matrix actually makes a picture of this life, actually it is not at all like this.

Ch 17 Breaking the chain of Mediocrity

Mediocrity.

It is a silent partner of the matrix, and most people fall into this matrix just because they are mediocre that is they are average and follow the herd. They are made to think like the tribe and follow the tribe, instead of actually doing something at their own and thinking out of the box.

The meaning of the word mediocre means an average person . Average, common and not extraordinary.

This mediocrity let's them follow into the trap, and as 95% of the people struggle in their life, they do the same.

Breaking this chain of mediocrity, a thinking of following of herd only, will let you get out of this trap and change your life.

Remember that you are not born to work in a factory, but to actually own that or to have a stake of ownership in that.

Rise above the ordinary.

Now what do I Mean?

Mediocrity is the comfort zone where people avoid risks, innovation, or critical thinking, and just simply follow the crowd.

But the actuall true success demands breaking free from this cycle.

Like, Many students aim for careers like becoming doctors, engineers, or government employees, not because they are passionate about these fields, but because they see these as "safe" options dictated by society.

Today in the craze of sports, I see a lot of my friends going to some or the other academy of any of the sports and aiming to become something out of that, but actually they also end up following the same one after 9th and follow that 4 streams after class 10.

You can understand this better with help of this story.

There is my one friend whose name was Dharya . He is also my uncle in relation. He is in class 11th as of 2024-25.

He is 3 years older than me, but we all in our neighbor had a group of some 5-6 friends, and in that he was also the one.
From a very early age only only he was fond of gaming and this content creation. He actually wanted to become that only.

But just because of his parents today he is following the same path, the mediocre one, by opting of Non - Medical and aiming to crack that prestigious "IIT", despite being good at something else.

I totally know that he is not one made at all for that field, but he is following that because of the society and parent's pressure. The in-built talent in him is destroyed and killed to follow the path of average people.

Similarly, while most of the students after choosing medical aim to become doctor or surgeon, there is my one friend who had some different plans to break the path of mediocrity, but he was not able to because of that same reasons.

His name was Arshdeep, he is currently in class 10th (2024-25) and he always wanted to choose medical and then do the diploma and courses on pharmaceuticals.

Like this he wanted to gain knowledge about medicine and open medicine shops and dispensary and do a business of selling medicines .
He was inspired about this by his one the uncles who was very successful in the same and had a very big empire.
But now today, again he also chooses Non -Medical just because of his parents.

Even Elon Musk's ventures, like Tesla and SpaceX, challenge mediocrity. Where others saw electric vehicles or space exploration as high-risk, he saw opportunity.

But today Tesla's market cap surpassed $1 trillion in 2021 which highlights the rewards of innovation and breaking the chain of mediocrity.

The actual fight against this system is not much about this system, but about the mediocrity.

Just imagine that you have the ability to make something at your own, you can literally do a invention, but you are not actually doing that and working under someone in the chase of a pay check.

Here you are an engineer, but problem is that you have degrees , but not skills.
You have the chance, but not the courage to actually do something at your own and just work in a company.

The problem with society also is that they feel proud to listen a package of 1 crores instead of a 100 million dollar company.

As achieving the goal of 1 crore packages is also 1 out 1000 similarly is 1 out of 100 of the 100 million dollar business.

Now choose at your own.
Do you want to stay or quit?
Do you want to die as a common man or do something extraordinary?
Do you want to leave bills, payments and loans for your future generations or build a empire for them?

Choose.
Because ;
Breaking free from mediocrity requires courage and critical thinking more than ambition , and a willingness to embrace uncertainty.

It starts with questioning societal norms, like your friend did, and finding unique opportunities that align with one's strengths and interests.

Success is not about following the herd but about carving your own path, taking calculated risks, and daring to dream big.

Those who rise above mediocrity understand that life is not a race to fit in but a journey to stand out.

Today I am also taking actions to achieve my goals despite being a 13 years old boy and despite my friends still dreaming of something, and I actually taking actions for the same.

Today also we have all this inventions and advanced technology because there was someone who broke that chain of mediocrity.

It's you who have to change you!

"Greatness begins where mediocrity end and a dare to challenge the ordinary, and you'll discover the extraordinary."

Unit 6 The Role of Government in Education

Education

Ch 18 The flawed governmental foundation

Now, We already know how this system was made and why the hell it was
made.

Just to produce loyal workforce, work under the powerful and more.
Now these all things happened in past while the colonial rule and before
1947 , our independence from the British.

But why we still today are so dumb that we haven't changed this system,
the government even after knowing the effects of this system.

See before this book also there are hundreds of time, people actually
pointing out the education system, and do you think that government don't
understands this?

Not at all. They know everything.

So why they don't bring a change? Why?
Are they deaf and dumb?
While they are. Who?
We.

Who are still in favor of the government and just raising up the mediocre
issues in front of government for our benefit, but what for society?

Education system.

We don't demand a good education system from them.
Never.

That is why we as a society fails and they - 'political' leader wins despite loosing as a human and "leader".
Rise up .
Break mediocrity.
Question these leaders, this system.
Really think for the country and the future ones.

We are just stressed upon to produce the bookish knowledge while exams and there is no space for practical learning.

The curriculum is rarely updated to match the pace of technological advancements or address pressing societal issues.

In a world driven by rapid innovation, this static approach leaves students ill-prepared for modern challenges.

The government has played a significant role in perpetuating these flaws. Poor policy implementation, inadequate teacher training, and corruption have weakened the education system's foundation.

Public schools, which cater to the majority of India's population, literally lack basic infrastructure, qualified teachers, and learning materials.

Instead of focusing on holistic development, education policies prioritize quantity over quality, with initiatives aimed more at increasing enrollment than improving learning outcomes.

This flawed foundation also creates significant socio-economic disparities.

The lack of proper education in rural and marginalized communities ensures that children from these areas remain trapped in poverty, unable to break free from systemic inequality.

Private institutions, on the other hand, cater to the elite, further widening the gap between the privileged and the underprivileged.

The consequences of this system are dire. India's youth, despite being one of the largest and most dynamic populations globally, struggle with unemployment.

Degrees, once considered a ticket to a brighter future are now just insufficient as they fail to reflect actual skills. Employers often find graduates lacking the practical abilities needed in today's industries.

This disconnect between education and employability not only hampers individual progress but also stunts national growth.

Moreover, the system's resistance to change perpetuates societal stagnation. While countries like Finland and Singapore continuously innovate their education models to nurture problem-solving and critical thinking, India clings to outdated methods.

The failure to adapt ensures that the nation's potential remains unrealized, creating a vicious cycle where future generations inherit the same flawed foundation.

To move forward, India must recognize the urgent need for systemic reform.
The government has the resources and responsibility to revolutionize the education system, yet political apathy and mismanagement prevail.

Until then, the flawed foundation will continue to weigh heavily on the nation, preventing it from rising to its true potential.

Countries like Singapore, Japan and Finland are something today because of its education only.

The system there is there to actually help people, but not destroy them. True education and the right education is the right of every citizen. Fight for it.

The role of government is far bigger than we think. In this unit we will discuss that only.

Ch 19 Uneducated leaders and misguided policies

Now first of all with the title of the chapter if you think, by educated I mean
that degree part and some that a mediocre one says, then you are wrong.

The political leaders of the country are not actually educated, like the biggest is that they are not leaders but they are 'political leaders'.

They actually don't bring a change because in their past they haven't realized the need to reform in this system just because everyone around them was the same, mediocre, and most importantly we as a society don't demand a good education system from them, because for us as a society the political agenda of religion and caste is more important than education and environment.

A good leadership in education is really-really important but unfortunately in our country the leadership is not seen because as it is not actually taught in the schools and universities.

Further corruption and stagnant policies by the leaders are the result of the education system only.

But do political leaders understand this?

Do they understand the need to reform?

For sure they no.

But again then the problem comes to us.

We while the time of elections focus on that freebies that the government
will provide after coming into action, the things they will do for our religion
and culture, the subsidies they will give and a protection from other
cultures will give us are the top priorities of ours as a society.

For us education, environment, health care is not important or if they are
important, they are more important than then the growth of our culture
and religion.

For us real growth lies in these areas, but not in terms of the areas where
we actually need.
Will this agenda of caste, religion, culture and all these things will actually
make us the "vishav guru"? Or the development of education, healthcare
facilities and environment will be the one making it?

If this same case of religion and culture existed in Shaheed Bhagat Singh ,
then do you think that we might today be getting the freedom we have
today from Britishers.

Do you know for him country was over his religion and culture and just
because of it he even portrayed himself as an atheist.

Bhagat Singh was born into a Sikh family and wore his turban on long hair,
which are sacred symbols of Sikhism.

Still, he placed the cause of India's independence above everything,
including his personal beliefs and cultural identity.

In 1928, after the murder of Lala Lajpat Rai during a peaceful protest,
Bhagat Singh and his associates decided to retaliate against the British
authorities.

They planned to assassinate James A. Scott, the police officer responsible for Lala Lajpat Rai's death. However, due to mistaken identity, they killed John Saunders, a different police officer.

To avoid capture, Bhagat Singh knew he had to change his appearance drastically. Since his long hair and turban were distinct identifiers, he made the deeply sacrificial decision to cut his hair and shave his beard—something that was deeply against Sikh practices and symbolic of his identity.
These were some of the things done by him for his country and we can't even just for the sake of the development of the society at an real level can change our minds.

I am definitely sure that God, Waheguru will be super happy with Bhagat Singh for all that he did for his country .

Can we also do something?

Here we have to only and only ask for a good education system, a healthy environment and a good healthcare system to really grow as a society and that's it.

After all of this a another problem comes within the system is corruption . Corruption within the education sector is another significant hurdle.

Reports of bribery in teacher recruitment, embezzlement of funds meant for school infrastructure, and manipulation of examination systems are not uncommon or new to us .

In some cases, funds allocated for building schools have been siphoned off, leaving projects incomplete and students deprived of basic facilities.

One glaring example is the misuse of funds in educational initiatives by certain state governments.

These programs, designed to improve infrastructure and quality, have been exploited for personal and political gains.

As a result, schools often boast impressive buildings but lack quality teaching staff, resources, or innovative curriculum.

The role of government in education is crucial, but it must be guided by competence, integrity, and a genuine commitment to public welfare.

Only then can India's education system evolve from a flawed foundation to a robust and inclusive framework that empowers its youth.

Ch 20 The Mediocre curriculum

If you will get a little closer and start analysing to the ground reality of curriculum then you will find that in our country the same universities are teaching the same topic and handing out the same number of degrees to the same number of people every single fucking year.

So, Why I am telling you to focus more on the development of education in the country than the culture?

Why?
Just one reason, that every single country in the world today which is developed like Japan, Singapore, Switzerland, Finland and US and UK are because of their education.

If our country also wants to become the same, then we have to focus on the education system and especially the curriculum, that what is taught to us.

This stagnant curriculum of the country not only fails to prepare students for future challenges but also perpetuates a system that values marks and degrees over true knowledge and skills.

If we have to build a good education system, then the government has to focus more on the development of curriculum rather than the infrastructure.

I know that the infrastructure of India is also where it sucks, but by building big institutions also we will not be able to something really big.

What will be the value if today in 10 institutions we are getting knowledge and in future that will go up to 100 institutions in the country, but most important if in these 100 institutions also we will be getting that mediocre education only then we will only produce more workers rather than true thinkers.

We have to build the most important thing first and that is the curriculum and then the process of giving knowledge.

The curriculum that sucks with outdated knowledge

The world has changed drastically in the past two decades like we have seen the development of 2G internet to 5G today and normal petrol and diseal cars to electric cars yet the Indian curriculum remains largely the same with no change in it.

Students are still taught knowledge that holds little relevance in today's context or almost nothing. Students like me are taught still the same thing in their computer science textbooks that how to use MS PowerPoint and MS Word in the age of AI, softwares and coding.

Also , we are expected to memorize formulas, historical dates, and lengthy definitions, even though these can be accessed in seconds through AI tools or the internet with just one click.

Like if I want to solve a mathematical problem too that can be done by chat gpt, so why I am being taught that how to solve that problem.

Simply , why the hell I am learning herons formula if my one real life
problem as an engineer to can be solved by AI and I then can use my brain
to create something big with the help of AI only.

Instead schools should teach me public speaking in the curriculum,
decision making, negotiations and more which can not be done through AI.

Instead of leveraging technology to foster innovation, schools force students
to spend years memorizing information that is readily available.
This approach stifles creativity and discourages critical thinking.

In contrast, countries like Finland and Singapore have embraced dynamic,
skill-based curricula. Finland, for instance, focuses on problem-solving,
collaboration, and real-world applications, making their students among
the best-prepared globally.

The Absence of real life skills

One of the most glaring shortcomings of the Indian education system is the
lack of real-life skills in the curriculum.

Financial literacy, for example, is a subject that every student should
master, yet it is rarely taught.

Students graduate without understanding how to manage money, invest
wisely, or budget effectively, leaving them ill-prepared for adulthood.

Similarly, using AI in work and creating something through it —a skill that
has become as essential as reading or writing in today's digital age—is
missing from most school syllabus. Emotional intelligence, communication,
and interpersonal skills are also ignored, even though these are critical for
personal and professional s

Consider the story of Ratan Tata, one of India's most humble business leaders.

Tata's success did not stem from blindly following the system but from thinking outside the box, taking calculated risks, and developing emotional intelligence.
His journey exemplifies the importance of skills over grades.

Now when it comes to skills they are nowhere because degrees and marks are more important for us.

In India, the importance placed on marks and degrees has overshadowed the pursuit of genuine knowledge and skills.

Students are judged not by their abilities or creativity but by their grades on a report card.
Just think that I can be taken into a job if I have a paper which has some value(in the system) and that shows that I am applicable of doing this, even if I don't actually know how to do it clearly and do it with a better understanding.

Just because of this, every day we hear a new news of fake degrees in media.
This misplaced emphasis creates a culture where schools prioritize completing the syllabus over imparting meaningful education, and colleges churn out graduates armed with degrees but lacking employable skills.

Despite spending years studying, these graduates find themselves ill-prepared for the job market, as they possess theoretical knowledge but lack real-world application.

Just because of this, Just a few months ago, TCS (Tata Consultancy Services Limited) has told that they had 80,000 Job vacancies, which is massive number in the form of vacancies especially for a company like TCS, because at one time it was said that in India TCS, Infosys are the companies that will hire anyone without looking at their skills or talents, but now the time had changed they are saying; we can find degrees but not

talents and skills in people, so how will we hire people and also why should
we?

Because of this a new wave of unemployment in the country is starting
where people are not getting jobs because they have degrees but not skills.

*"There is no need of collage degree because that don't teach you the real life
skills" - Elon Musk*

When people like Elon Musk don't send their children to normal schools
and build a school at their own for their children and their staff, where
their children can learn and do what they love and in which they are good,
then why we stress upon the normal education which don't pays us off.

The importance of ground level knowledge

Should I learn the history of my own country first , or of some other
country ,
like both are telling me about the politics and socialism, but what is your
view?

Like, Today students like me are burdened with memorizing historical
events like the French Revolution and Russian Revolution while remaining
ignorant of their own country's transformative events, such as the Green
Revolution and White Revolution.

These revolutions were pivotal in making India self-reliant in food and milk
production but they are barely touched upon in textbooks.

Even worse, there is no effort to teach students about the pressing issues in
their own regions, such as the traffic chaos in Bengaluru, the sewage
mismanagement in Gurgaon, or the slums in Mumbai, like this is true that
the students of these areas can see this at their won, but still if in textbooks
some solutions and stories can be included,then a change can be expected
by the new generation.

By neglecting ground-level realities, the system deprives students of the knowledge and tools needed to address these problems and become agents of change.

The worst part here is that we are taught knowledge all over the world despite that having no use in our life .

Instead if students will be taught about the events and knowledge around their area then the problems in the country can be solved with a fast pace than it is taking time today.

The stagnation of India's curriculum is not just a failure of the education system but a failure of imagination.

Real change requires a complete overhaul, from the content of textbooks to the methods of teaching. Schools must focus on imparting skills, fostering creativity, and preparing students for real-world challenges.

The government, too, has a critical role to play. Policies should prioritize skill-based learning, vocational training, and technology integration. Teachers must be trained to adapt to new methodologies, and curricula must be updated regularly to reflect societal and technological changes.

As Albert Einstein once said, "Education is not the learning of facts, but the training of the mind to think."

The government's role in maintaining a broken education system cannot be overlooked. Whether through complacency, corruption, or deliberate design, the system continues to prioritize compliance over creativity, ensuring a steady flow of low-skilled labor rather than innovators and entrepreneurs.

India must embrace this philosophy to create an education system that empowers its students to dream big, think differently, and lead the world into a brighter future.

Only then can we break free from the shackles of the stagnant curriculum and unlock the true potential of our nation.

Unit 7 Solutions
Ch 21 A global model for education

Now comes the most important part of the book.
Solutions.

How and what sort of a good education system should be?

See before explaining you the education system I personally want to be
established, I want you all to first know about the education systems
around the world through which ,we can really understand that how a good

education system should be by the help of the countries which are really good at their education system.

This is because by taking inspiration from the most successful education systems around the world, we can create a revolutionary global model.

This model combines the best practices from countries like Finland, Singapore, Switzerland, Estonia, Japan and Norway by ensuring that students are not only well-educated but also prepared to thrive in a complex and interconnected world of today.

Like this the things that I will mention will not seem as blind shots to you but actually that will be the practical things that have taken place in some part of the world.

We have to remember the words of Albert Einstein that are as follows:-
"Education is Not the Learning of Facts But the Training of the Mind to Think".

Student centric learning

In this students will actually get the chances of individual growth.
Now this is something that seems impractical in a country like India with a vast population, but it is not impossible.

Here instead of focusing on standardized tests, in Finland the teachers prioritize that each student should get the knowledge according to his own Interests.
In past in ancient India too the gurus did the same thing.

Now today we have to just bring down the student teacher ratio and half of the things are solved.

 Because in the classes too a teacher knows personally about 15 students out of the 45.

So still this is not that big deal.

In this system, the emphasis shifts from relentless exams and standardized testing to stress-free learning environments that nurture creativity and curiosity.

Instead of forcing students to conform to a rigid curriculum, education would be tailored to individual strengths, interests, and aspirations. By doing so, students would not only excel academically but also develop a lifelong love for learning.

Finland's success in creating happy, innovative students has proven that prioritizing well-being and individuality leads to better outcomes, both personally and professionally.

Finland's education system even highlights the importance of collaboration, critical thinking, and problem-solving over rote memorization.

Students are encouraged to question, analyze, and deeply understand concepts rather than memorize facts, with group projects and peer collaboration by encouraging teamwork and communication.

Real-life problems are integrated into the curriculum to teach practical application, and critical thinking skills are nurtured by promoting independent thought and reasoned arguments.

This is something that can be easily developed if the focus should not on that every single student should be solving the same problem separately, they should be encouraged for team work and this all should be organised like a competition.

 And the students should be divided into teams.

Additionally, education is completely free from preschool to university for all citizens and residents, covering tuition, textbooks, meals, and even transportation by ensuring universal access and equity regardless of socio-economic background.

Now how this can be done?

This is not something really difficult for the government, instead a really easy solution. How?

The government, instead of spending millions on the security of that politicians, giving free bies like anything that the money they have is something earned by them. (Tax)

Just there should be a shift too giving free education at least till class 8. As a result Finland is one of the happiest countries in the world with ranking low in stress levels and depression.

Also it ranks in the top 5 countries with the best education system around the world.

Skill based education

To ensure that students are equipped for the demands of the modern workforce, the global model incorporates Singapore's focus on skill-based education.
This is something that is lacking in almost 75% of the countries on the globe.

Students are being taught the topics that have no use in future and they even not meet the demands of today's world.

This is something that is been tackled by a global innovation hub like Singapore.

Singapore emphasizes a balance between foundational subjects (math, science) and modern skills like coding and AI.

Subjects like financial literacy, artificial intelligence, coding, and emotional intelligence are mandatory that prepares the students for the rapidly evolving job market.

These all are the things that are needed in today's world and will have high demand in future.

Integration of real-world applications into teaching, such as entrepreneurial challenges and STEM projects is also a part of Singapore's education system.
Moreover, the curriculum would emphasize real-world problem-solving and entrepreneurial projects, encouraging students to think critically and develop practical solutions to global challenges.

This shift from theoretical knowledge to actionable skills ensures that students are not just educated but also empowered to make meaningful contributions to society.

As a result, even despite being a small country it is one the most developed country in the world with also constantly ranking high in education rankings.

For this, the countries have to shift their focus from the current ways of learning and teaching to the new ones for the development of the society.

Equal Opportunity Through Vocational and Academic Balance

Switzerland offers equal access to high-quality education for all the students in their country, regardless of socio-economic status and their background.

This is again a big deal that is lacking in our country, like in our country the poor even don't have access to basic education and the middle class are now being unable to afford the cost of education in the country.

After making the system better, we have to even make sure that every child in the country is able to access the education.

Switzerland has set an example for other countries by adopting a dual system of education which involves vocational training and academic education.

Now what is this?
Vocational Training.

Students spend part of their week working in a real job setting (e.g., as apprentices in industries like IT, engineering, or healthcare). This gives them hands-on experience and helps them develop practical skills relevant to their chosen field and learn by experience rather than reading .

Academic Education.
The rest of the week is spent in school learning theoretical subjects such as mathematics, science, and communication, which complement their vocational training.

This is something that I personally wanted to have in all the countries.

Just because the students will not be like a robot who are trained for a specific task, but they will be the real critical thinkers who will be using their critical thinking skills to innovate.

This system ensures that students not only gain a solid theoretical foundation but also develop practical skills, making them job-ready while still allowing them to pursue higher education if they choose.

 It creates a strong link between education and the labor market, reducing unemployment and ensuring a skilled workforce.

As a result it's education system consistently ranks in the top 5 in the world and also they rank at 1st position in the whole world when it comes to innovation.

Global awareness and sustainability

In today's world, students must be equipped to address global challenges. And they will be able to do this if they will be having a global awareness of it.
Norway incorporates climate change education and sustainability into its curriculum.

Schools would partner with global organizations to offer exchange programs, virtual collaborations, and community projects, fostering a sense of global citizenship among students.

By instilling these values early on, the education system would cultivate a generation of socially responsible leaders who prioritize the well-being of the planet and its people.

Like here they are not only giving them the theoretical knowledge about environment, but also collaborating with companies and organizations that helps the students to understand the need to sustain with one step ahead.

Use of technology in education

Japan a leader in tech and AI.
We know this , but how they are actually at this level?
Japan incorporates AI-powered learning systems to deliver personalized lessons by adjusting the pace and difficulty based on each student's needs.

Robots are used in classrooms for collaborative learning and language practice.
For Example, The Sota robot in Japan helps students improve their English speaking skills through interactive lessons.

Schools use AI tools like adaptive learning platforms to help struggling students catch up or challenge advanced learners.

Now Japan needs no introduction when it comes to innovation and technology.

Just because of this they tackle every single problem in their country and constantly rank high .

Even Japan is a country which has taken a pioneer step in teacher training programs.

As already discussed in the book teachers don't get respect in this system, but Japan had some new plans and they give a lot of respect to the teachers of their country and had even given them a tag of "national heroes".

Teachers who are bound by the curriculum and pressured by school administration, often emphasize exam preparation over holistic education.

Schools, in turn, are driven by their need to maintain high rankings and reputations, which are typically measured by their student's academic achievements.

This is a cycle that is tackled by Japan and it leads to the betterment of the society at an big level.

Summing up

If suming up all the things then a education system should have :-

Dynamic Curriculums that are regularly updated to include emerging fields like AI, sustainability, and global studies.

Holistic Evaluation by replacing standardized tests with project-based and skill-based assessments.

Teacher Empowerment like, Competitive salaries, continuous professional development, and societal respect for educators.

Vocational Respect for equal emphasis on academic and vocational training paths.

Global Collaboration to encourage exchange programs, international projects, and global problem-solving initiatives.

Mental Health First; There should be a mandatory counseling and mental health programs in all schools.

Equal Opportunity for akk the students by Free education for all, minimizing the gap between urban and rural education.

Skill-Based Learning that will Include financial literacy, emotional intelligence, and entrepreneurship in the curriculum.

Reduced Academic Pressure by Limiting homework and school hours to prioritize well-being and extracurricular exploration.

Ch 22 The changes needed in education centres

Today we live in a world where every single things has experienced a change, weather it's our cars, internet, mobiles, the structure of homes and almost everything as we know.

But again this fucking system has a problem that this remains same and the same.

As in the previous chapter we have discussed how the nation's can make the best education system by learning from each other, but in this chapter I have my some personal beliefs that a education system should be like this, and it has again got the inspiration from the global education systems.

Which are that ones? My beliefs?

1) From the starting of the chapter only we have got one thing to know that the past education system was far more better than the current one, where there was no system of textbooks and rote memorization.

Except the caste system there was everything super fine in this system (gurukul) So just keep the caste system aside and take this as a standard. So today also we have to take inspiration from the past education system before the industrialization that was really benefiting all of us.

2) The education should not be a system of profit. It's shouldn't be a business.
Like I am a person who totally believes in a capitalist mindset but I also know that education shouldn't be a business.

3) Seeking knowledge and developing yourself should not be a system of competition and it should be purely based upon gaining knowledge and becoming a wise man.

4) Theoretical learning must be transitioned to digital platforms like YouTube, Coursera, and AI-powered tools like chat gpt that can provide students with access to a wealth of information, tutorials, and lectures from experts around the world.

These platforms make theoretical knowledge accessible, customizable, and engaging, allowing students to learn at their own pace.
With theory moved online, classroom time can be repurposed for active engagement.
Discussions, debates, and problem-solving sessions can dominate the academic schedule, enabling students to convert theoretical concepts into real-world applications.

For instance, instead of passively learning about renewable energy in a classroom, students could design and test their own solar panels or wind turbines.

5) Just because of the same reason government should focus upon providing internet access in every part of the country.

6) Education must prioritize practical implementation. Labs, workshops, and field trips should become the foundation of the learning process. Students should engage in hands-on activities, work on real-world projects, and tackle challenges that mirror the complexities of life outside academia.

7) The role of educators in this transformed system is pivotal.
Teachers and professors must evolve from traditional lecturers to mentors and facilitators. Their primary responsibility would be to guide students in applying their knowledge creatively and effectively.
Instead of merely delivering lectures, educators would lead interactive sessions, provide constructive feedback, and help students navigate the challenges of their projects.

For example, a science teacher could mentor students in designing a water purification system for a local community, while a business professor might guide students in developing a sustainable startup idea.

8) Also all the students solving the same problem separately, they should be encouraged to team up and solve it as a team.
Evaluate students based on their creativity, collaboration, and problem-solving skills through projects, portfolios, and presentations.

9) Redesign curriculums to spark curiosity and encourage students to be lifelong learners.
Move away from rigid curriculums to dynamic, evolving courses that adapt to the world's changing needs.
Collaborate with industries, businesses, and community organizations to provide students with internships, apprenticeships, and real-world experiences.

10) Introduce entrepreneurship as part of the curriculum. Teach students how to identify opportunities, take calculated risks, and develop innovative solutions, encouraging them to create rather than consume.
Implement digital tools like AI, VR, and online platforms to make education more interactive and accessible.
Use technology to transition theoretical knowledge online, freeing up classroom time for discussions and practical work.

The ultimate goal is to create a world where education empowers every individual to reach their potential, contribute meaningfully to society, and address the challenges of tomorrow with confidence and competence.

 This is the education system the world needs to embrace , one that placed humanity and progress at its core.

Ch 23 The Mindset shift needed in parents, society and students itself

Do the change in all these things and this whole system will solve the problem?
Will it help us achieve the goal that we want to after changing this system?
Ask yourself especially if you are a student.

The answer is of course No.

The transformation of this education system is totally incomplete without a fundamental shift in the mindset of parents, society, and students itself. Like even if we have solved the problem of corruption in the political system but still there are people in the society still using it as a tool to get out of from some of the problems then the change is incomplete.

Similarly here is the case with the mindset.
If we will change that mindset that we have as a whole bunch of society then the problem can be solved even if the system isn't.

Now what are the changes that we need ?
See as discussing about every aspect earlier in the book itself, the problematic one, then I think so that there is not much need about telling you all what we have to do; parents know, society knows what the hell can be one but still I will tell the top of the things that we have to do.

But most importantly as a student, be with me in this chapter.

I can be a bit bitter, I can bit rude, I can be sarcastic, but listen, because I have figured what the hell I have to do and how I will do and for the same I have started taking actions but now it's your turn .

Even, I also don't like when people say all this about that gen Z that they are like this and this is their future, but that's the reality check that we have to accept and then prove them wrong, but how that will happen?

"By changing and focusing on the thing that you have between your ears and not you legs".

By focusing on yourself and not your friends and the opposite sex around you.
By focusing upon your goals and actions and not your fathers money that he has earned by doing hardwork.

But before that let's see the changes in mindset of parents and society needed.

The mindset shift in parents

1. Focus on Learning, Not Marks
The Current Mindset of the parents are like this that Marks and ranks define success and they are the parameters to define their child by it, but it's not.
Instead a shift that is needed is like; Emphasize understanding, creativity, and skill development over grades. Ask, "What did you learn today?" instead of "What marks did you get?"

2. Support Interests, Not Expectations
The Current Mindset - Parents push careers like medicine, engineering, or law as they are the mediocre ones, and they don't actually see the real need of the child.
The Shift Needed is like that parents should Encourage their child to explore their passions, even in unconventional fields.
Success is more likely when kids love what they do and which they want their career to be started in.

3. Value Skills Over Degrees
Current Mindset: Degrees are the ultimate goal.

Shift Needed: Promote skill acquisition, practical knowledge, and real-world problem-solving.
Teach children to learn things that matter in today's dynamic world.

4. Encourage Failure as Growth
Current Mindset: Failure is bad and should be avoided at all costs.
Shift Needed: Teach that failure is a stepping stone to success. Celebrate efforts and resilience rather than just results. This will help children develop grit and perseverance.

5. Model Lifelong Learning
Current Mindset: Learning is limited to school years.
Shift Needed: Show children that learning never stops.
Parents should demonstrate curiosity, learn new skills, and adapt to changes.

This creates an environment where growth is continuous.
This is something that every billionaire and successful person too tells to do, that you should never stop learning.
Because the most beautiful thing about knowledge is that no one can take it from you.

6) The change in the definition of success
Success should no longer be defined by grades and degrees but by skills, passion, and contributions to the society.
Parents should celebrate every milestone that showcases their child's growth and capabilities either that are academic or outside it .

The midset shift in the society

1. Break the Cycle of Judgment and Comparison
Current Reality: Society thrives on judging individuals based on grades, income, or career status, leading to pressure and low self-esteem.
Shift Needed: Embrace individuality and stop comparing children based on a rigid scale of success. Celebrate diverse talents, whether in academics, arts, or entrepreneurship.

2. Shift Focus from Stability to Growth
Current Reality: Society values stable jobs (government, engineering, etc.) over dynamic careers that involve risk or innovation.
Shift Needed: Teach that growth, adaptability, and lifelong learning are more important than static, "secure" careers. Encourage youth to explore fields like technology, startups, and freelancing.

3. Move from Gender Stereotypes to Equal Opportunities
Current Reality: Society often imposes roles and expectations based on gender (e.g., boys in STEM, girls in caregiving roles).
Shift Needed: Normalize all genders pursuing any career or interest without societal judgment. Support equal pay, representation, and leadership opportunities.

4. Stop Romanticizing Struggle and Hardship
Current Reality: Society glorifies the "struggling hero" narrative, expecting people to sacrifice health and happiness to achieve success.
Shift Needed: Normalize self-care, mental health support, and balanced living. Success should not come at the cost of well-being.As there is no need of 60-70 hour work week.

5. Eliminate the Stigma Around Failure
Current Reality: Failure is viewed as shameful, and those who fail face societal ostracization.
Shift Needed: Teach that failure is a natural step toward success and

innovation. Encourage resilience and learning from mistakes.

The mindset shift in my dear friends (students)

If you are still reading than you might be saying that What the Fuck is this education system.

This has just destroyed us, whereas we should get a better opportunity to learn and understand.

All the things discussed till now are something that all the other pillars like parents, teachers, government, schools and society should see for us, we soft ones!

But now wake up, if a person like me might be writing this book 15-20 years ago, then you all were the dear ones, but not today.

Today a lot of problems are with you all only.
Today your parents are not exactly like that, society is not the same and even government is trying to bring a change at some point but they are sleeping.
But now here you all are the problem.

Do you even think that this system should be changed for you all and the future who are even better than you?

Really?
Better and you and they more better?
See yourself.

Do you even respect the luxury and facilities that the 2 people in your life are giving to you to whom you say parents?

Are you even the one working upon your goals?

Are you struggling to achieve something or to get something from your parents and friends?

Or you are struggling to find a better girlfriend/boyfriend like your friend?
Or you are still not respecting your parents because you expected them to be more rich as your friend's parents?

What are the struggles and challenges with you?
You are getting everything and still not respecting it.
Wanting to achieve your goals but not working on it.

Some being just opposite of if who are just into textbooks and learning every single thing but not the one which will help them in future, the so called fucking toppers.

Actually you are not using the power of your mind correctly that is invisible and not using the most powerful power today correctly that is visible and that is on your tips - your smartphones.

See , there is nothing that can control you until you give someone or something a chance to do so.

Social media, internet, AI anything even the boy or girl to whom you like, can't control until you give the chance.

Today you have every single recourse with you but not using it correctly? Not using social media, internet and AI correctly.

If today I am writing a book and really working on my goals it's just because of these things and not just because of them but by actually working and taking actions and not just dreaming of the life that I want.

Not getting inspired by that fake reels of business or IIT's and actually working on something valuable by using technology and books rightly.

If today Gen Z's like Mr Beast , Iman Gadzhi, Ishan Sharma , Noah Beck, Sophia Kianni or Raj Shamani, they are not ones using Social media and intrenet like you all and just dreaming of their future life and even not taking actions to achieve something .

They are the ones taking actions and having patience in them and have the courage to do hard work and take real risks.

If you don't know about them,all the names that I mentioned except Mr Beast so search them on google and you will be shocked.

 I am also sure you might be knowing about peope like Carry Minati, Bhuvan Bham, Ishow speed, Techno Gamers, Elvish Yadav , BTS, Andrew

Tate and all sort of these people whose content is not actually that will make you someone better but will just ruin you.

I know they have also done a lot of hardwork in their life but it's not that you will follow them instead follow people like that I mentioned .

Here if talking about hardwork that it is something that is even done by a person who is finally building up his dream house and the one working to make his dream house, it's upon what you want to choose.

Either the house owner or construction worker.

Today your smart phone is like something that of AK 47 which you can either use to scare people and become a gangster or be a hero for them like a soldier.
You have to choose at your own.

Today I am not just getting inspired by actually becoming a business man but actually working on that only from today itself , class 8 and not waiting for the future until I will turn 18 and then do something.

Even not just having a fake dream because of social media because if today I will go to my father who for the sake is business man , but actually a shop

keeper, he will just slap me because he will not understand what type of business I want to do and how I want to do.
Instead today I am writing this book then selling it online and having 3-4 steps earlier to start my business at my own business by my own capital and personal brand in hand.

Today my half of the friends want to be a business man or a stock trader, but don't know what the hell is bearish and bullish market and don't what the hell is ROI and equity.

Then there are some who know everything from A to Z about business and life but still waiting to pass class 10 and turn 18 and then do something and currently just chilling on fathers money by having big dreams .

Shift your mindset.

Today a teenager like me who wants to actually do something big in his life by not actually dreaming but actually doing, read books based on self help, psychology, business, finance, investing and biographies and autobiographies and make the notes of the books, and use the learning of that at the ground level.

Follow channels on YouTube based on the same topic , listen podcasts and read articles and news on in shorts, BBC and Forbes every day.

If you want to make your parents proud then shift the focus.
Now comes the main point, mindset shift.

I don't think so you need to know much more but still look after all of this.

1) From Consumption to Creation
Current Mindset: Using social media for endless scrolling and entertainment.
Shift: Leverage social media to build a personal brand, network, or create content that adds value.

2. From Grades to Skills
Current Mindset: Focusing solely on getting high marks.
Shift: Prioritize learning practical skills like coding, digital marketing, or public speaking that can directly lead to opportunities.

3. From Competition to Collaboration
Current Mindset: Treating peers as competitors in academics.
Shift: Collaborate with others, share ideas, and build connections to grow collectively.

4. From Rote Learning to Critical Thinking
Current Mindset: Memorizing facts and data for exams.
Shift: Develop the ability to analyze, question, and solve real-world problems creatively.

5. From Instant Gratification to Long-Term Vision
Current Mindset: Seeking quick results and rewards (e.g., viral posts, gaming).
Shift: Focus on long-term goals like building a career, mastering a skill, or creating a meaningful project.

6. From Entertainment to Education on Social Media
Current Mindset: Watching only entertainment or gossip.
Shift: Follow pages, channels, or influencers who provide valuable insights into careers, skills, and entrepreneurship.

7. From Fear of Failure to Embracing Growth
Current Mindset: Avoiding challenges due to fear of failing.
Shift: View failures as learning opportunities and an essential part of success.

8. From Being Busy to Being Productive
Current Mindset: Spending hours on scrolling.
Shift: Focus on time management, prioritizing high-impact activities like learning a new language, freelancing, or joining meaningful extracurriculars.

9. From Knowledge Accumulation to Skill Application
Current Mindset: Collecting information from books and encyclopedias but not applying it.
Shift: Experiment with what you learn – build projects, solve real-world problems, or teach others.

10. From Fixed to Growth Mindset
Current Mindset: Believing that intelligence or talent is fixed (e.g., "I'm not good at math").
Shift: Adopt the belief that with effort and practice, any skill can be learned and improved.

At last change mindsets like having girlfriend- boyfriend, scrolling social media, getting in FOMO after seeing friends, chilling on fathers money and all that you can understand.

Develop everyday skills like journaling, tracking your goals and making actionable plans and working on the goals.

Then at last follow the content which will make you grow.

See, that before my this book also as told to you, people have tried to bring a change in this system, but still it's there itself.

So I want you to get out of this as early, develop yourself and just make your parents proud, because till the time you are locked in this mediocrity and education system, you can't be successful.

People who are something today, they are just because of that they have escaped this and not by being in this.

End Thoughts

Let me make one thing clear to all of you; I am not against education.

On the contrary, I deeply value the role of education and literacy in shaping who we are and that is something that we have discussed in the introduction of the book too, even If I have been able to write this book, it is only because I am educated and literate.

My issue is not with education itself but with the education system that is something that I wanted to convey through this book.

The current system, with its outdated structure and rigid methods, is not designed to nurture curiosity, creativity, or real-world skills which we have already discussed.

Schools and colleges just focus on ticking boxes , passing exams, securing degrees, and chasing marks.

But do life is the same?
Life is dynamic, unpredictable, and full of challenges that require skills far beyond what is taught in the classroom.
Life doesn't operate in check boxes.

Instead of making schools a place of stress and competition, they should be places of joy and exploration.

Students should go to school not just to attend classes but to learn in the true sense of the word learning by doing, experiencing, experimenting, and participating in activities that spark their interests.

Competitions, projects, and networking should take center stage, fostering collaboration and innovation.

Even if you excel academically, don't limit yourself to exams alone explore Olympiads, participate in diverse competitions, and build real-world skills that set you apart.

Success is not guaranteed by marks or degrees.
Schools train students to conform, preparing them for jobs rather than empowering them to escape mediocrity.

Look at people like Sundar Pichai, Satya Nadella, or Alakh Pandey they succeeded not because they stayed within the system but because they learned to think beyond it.

They didn't just follow the path laid out for them; they created their own.

The system, as it stands, is designed to churn out employees, not innovators or entrepreneurs.

But if we want to build a generation that truly excels, we need to focus on skills like problem-solving, critical thinking, and handling pressure.

Exams do have value , like they teach us how to work under stress and solve problems in limited time but that's just one aspect of life. Education should go beyond exams and grades.

Even if exams are able to teach to handle pressure and make decisions in limited time, that's also something not taught in this system, and the only focus is on getting marks.

Life is too short to be confined by a system that doesn't cater to individual potential.

It's time to shift our perspective, to redefine education as a journey of growth and empowerment rather than a race for marks and degrees.

Escape the matrix of mediocrity.

Think big, learn beyond the classroom, and focus on building a life filled with meaning and impact.

This book is not a critique of education itself but a call to revolutionize the way we educate, learn, and grow.

Let's create an education system that truly prepares us for life and not for exams.